BRINGING THE
CLOUD
DOWN TO EARTH

How to choose, launch, and get the most from cloud solutions for your business

Rhonda Abrams:

**facebook.com/
RhondaAbramsSmallBusiness**

twitter.com/RhondaAbrams

PlanningShop:

facebook.com/PlanningShop

twitter.com/PlanningShop

Bringing the Cloud Down to Earth
How to choose, launch, and get the most from cloud solutions for your business

Free business tips and information:
To receive PlanningShop's free email newsletter on starting and growing a successful business, sign up at www.PlanningShop.com.

PlanningShop:
555 Bryant Street, #180
Palo Alto, CA 94301 USA

650-364-9120
Fax: 650-364-9125
Email: info@PlanningShop.com
www.PlanningShop.com

PlanningShop is a division of Rhonda, Inc., a California corporation.

Acknowledgments:
Contributing writing and research: Alice LaPlante, Anne Marie Bonneau
Editing: Rebecca Gaspar
Proofreading: Mark Woodworth
Cover and interior design: Diana Russell, www.DianaRussellDesign.com
Illustrations: April Milne
Indexing: Sandi Schroeder, Schroeder Indexing Services
Rhonda Abrams's photos: cover, Garrett Hubbard; page iv, Christopher Briscoe

ISBN: 978-1-933895-29-1 (ebook)

ISBN 10: 1-933895-34-9 (print)

ISBN 13: 978-1-933895-34-5 (print)

Library of Congress Control Number: 2012930256

"This publication is designed to provide accurate and authoritative information in regard to the subject matter covered. It is sold with the understanding that the publisher and author are not engaged in rendering legal, accounting, or other professional services. If legal advice or other expert assistance is required, the services of a competent professional person should be sought."

— from a Declaration of Principles jointly adopted by a committee of the American Bar Association and a committee of publishers.

Printed in Canada

10 9 8 7 6 5 4 3 2 1

Bringing the Cloud Down to Earth

Rhonda Abrams
USA Today columnist
and best-selling author of
*Successful Business Plan:
Secrets & Strategies*

About the Author

Entrepreneur, author, and nationally syndicated columnist Rhonda Abrams is widely recognized as a leading expert on entrepreneurship and small business. Rhonda's column for *USA Today*, "Successful Strategies," is the most widely distributed column on small business and entrepreneurship in the United States, reaching tens of millions of readers each week.

Rhonda's books have been used by millions of entrepreneurs. Her first book, *Successful Business Plan: Secrets & Strategies*, is the best-selling business plan guide in America. It was named one of the top 10 business books for entrepreneurs by both *Forbes* and *Inc.* magazines. She is also the author of more than a dozen other books on entrepreneurship and has sold more than a million copies of her books. Rhonda's other books are perennial best-sellers, with three of them having reached the nationally recognized "Top 50 Business Bestseller" list.

Rhonda not only writes about business—she lives it! As the founder of three successful companies, Rhonda has accumulated an extraordinary depth of experience and a real-life understanding of the challenges facing entrepreneurs. Rhonda first founded a management consulting practice working with clients ranging from one-person start-ups to Fortune 500 companies. An early web pioneer, she founded a website for small business that she later sold. In 1999, Rhonda started a publishing company—now called PlanningShop—focusing exclusively on topics of business planning, entrepreneurship, and new business development. PlanningShop is America's leading academic publisher focusing exclusively on entrepreneurship.

A popular public speaker, Rhonda regularly addresses leading industry and trade associations, business schools, and corporate conventions and events. Educated at Harvard University and UCLA, Rhonda lives in Palo Alto, California.

Finding Value in the Cloud

By Michael Dell

If you are about to read this book, then you're already interested in the amazing possibilities of cloud computing. What can moving to the cloud mean to your business? Is the technology really proven? What kind of investment will you need to make? How do you get started?

More than a quarter century ago, I founded Dell because I believed in the power of technology to help individuals and businesses better achieve their full potential. Back then, it was about PCs and ever-increasing compute power. Today, it's about how technological breakthroughs like cloud computing can give small- and medium-sized companies access to enterprise-class applications and IT resources in a way that helps reduce cost and free up resources.

It's an exciting time for all of us. We're standing at the threshold of a revolution, one characterized by the urgency of unlimited expectations. The convergence of mobility and connectivity has created a demand for immediate access to applications and data anywhere, anytime. I call this "Yes, Now" computing. The cloud can give us what we need, when we need it, exactly how we want it.

We need to think about cloud as an enabler of real-world business results—from driving operational efficiencies to increasing employee productivity to improving the bottom line to giving you that competitive edge you need to grow and thrive. That's where the real value lies.

Who This Book Is For

You need *Bringing the Cloud Down to Earth* if...

- Your ears are ringing from all the hype about cloud computing, yet despite the online blurbs, radio spots, and television ads, you still don't get what the cloud means for your business.

- You're hearing about the wonderful ways the cloud is making companies more efficient, but you don't know if it's right for your company.

- You and your employees and contractors need to be able to work when not physically in the office, but you can't access the business information you need from home or from on the road.

- You need to do some major upgrades on your software or hardware, but coming up with the cash—or cash flow—is a challenge.

- You want to make sure any move to the cloud can be done without major disruptions to critical on-site applications you intend to keep and use during the transition.

- You're sold on the idea of moving your data and some applications to the Internet, but you don't know how to choose the right solutions.

- You just want to know what all the fuss is about.

What is "The Cloud?"

By the end of this chapter...

you'll understand what the cloud is, and why businesses like yours are finding it so attractive.

Technology Transforms Business

There's no question that technology has changed the business world—bringing greater power, speed, and information as well as creating new business opportunities. Technology makes it possible for you to have much more information available to you, much faster, increasing the likelihood that you'll make smarter business decisions and serve your customers better. Technology also makes it easier to share that information and to communicate faster, easier, and cheaper.

Today, a new technology is on the horizon. Cloud-based computing, often simply referred to as "the cloud," represents a true paradigm shift.

Cloud computing can transform your business. Because of greater processing speed and bandwidth, many of the things you do in your office can now be done remotely, over the Internet. And while this seems just a simple thing, it means you have access to far greater power, with much less overhead and fewer complications.

"The cloud" is more than merely a buzzword, and more than simply this year's tech fad. It presents you with the opportunity to run your business more efficiently, while enjoying numerous options on business processes, applications, and services. It enables you to put your resources toward what you do best, rather than spending so much time and money managing your infrastructure. Cloud computing lets you run as efficiently as much bigger businesses, because you now have access to technoogy tools that previously were too expensive for your budget.

If you're just starting out, cloud computing puts a broad range of business applications at your fingertips without the upfront capital investment. Instead of having to purchase your own hardware and software and then hire someone to install and take care of it, you get the functionality you need provided as a service. You use what you need, when you need it, and you only pay for what you use. In short: You get all the computing power you require, but with more options and flexibility, and without the hassle or upfront costs.

Cloud Basics

The cloud. By now, you've been amply exposed to it. You've heard radio ads about it, seen billboards, read articles in the trade and business press. But you would still be excused if you didn't quite grasp what the cloud *is.* That's because companies are so intent on selling you cloud-based products that they rush past providing basic definitions.

There's an overwhelming amount of information about the cloud these days. Much of it can be bewildering, as all sorts of companies scramble to offer cloud-based offerings. This book will filter through the noise to help you understand and take full advantage of the cloud as it makes sense for *your* business. No nonsense, no jargon—just what you need to know to be productive.

factoid

In 1961, Stanford professor John McCarthy was one of the first to suggest a time-share, service bureau computing model.

At its most basic level, the cloud offers you computing resources—applications, file storage and sharing, and processing power—that *you access over the Internet*, from a distance. You can use these resources even though they are not residing on hardware (computers or servers) in your business or home. You use your computer, smartphone, or tablet, or indeed any "smart" device, to tap into those resources over the Internet.

JOURNEY TO THE CLOUD: GETTING STARTED

At this, the very beginning of your journey to the cloud, you should be taking an inventory of all the software applications you use, determining the necessary functional features of those applications, and beginning to perform your due diligence on the available cloud-based alternatives.

The opposite of a cloud-based computing resource is an *on-premise* resource (that's a word you should remember). With on-premise computing resources (software applications, data storage, email, and the like) you—or someone within your organization or an outside consultant you hire—have to choose, maintain, upgrade, and integrate all your business-related technology. Maintaining an on-premise computing environment is a big challenge, and often an expensive one, that can cause headaches and lead to serious tech emergencies and even business losses.

That's where the cloud comes in. Cloud service providers maintain, upgrade, manage, and sometimes even integrate your computing needs and business applications. All you have to do is turn on your computer (or tablet or other device), connect over the Internet and you have the power and data you need. You can "turn on" and "turn off" resources as needed. Cloud services tend to cost less than on-premise solutions as well. You pay a regular, predictable fee rather than purchasing upfront. Plus, because it's so easy for their customers to switch to a competitor if unhappy, cloud companies have a strong incentive to provide superior service and support. All this is good news for small and medium businesses.

Here's an example most people can relate to: Netflix. The movie rental company had tremendous early success renting DVDs by mail. You paid a monthly fee for the right to order movies, which were mailed to you. After viewing them, you mailed them back in special postage-prepaid envelopes. You got access to an incredibly large library of titles from the convenience of your home, and never paid another late fee to the local video rental store. Today, however, Netflix earns an increasingly large share of its revenue another way: through the cloud. Instead of having DVDs sent to you, you get instant access to many of the movies you want over the Internet— they are "streamed" directly to your computer (or television, or other device). The movies are no longer in your house, in your DVD player. They reside, and are played, in the cloud, and delivered over the Internet.

Now, let's look at an increasingly common business example of the cloud: data backup. Everyone agrees you should backup the data on your computer hard drive to prevent critical business information from being lost, stolen, or destroyed. In the past, this required physically copying data from individual computers or servers onto a storage backup device— usually a tape drive—on a regular basis. Then, that backup

learn the lingo

CLOUD COMPUTING: The delivery over the Internet of computing resources, such as processing power, storage capacity, or software functionality. Similar to the way that utilities such as electricity or gas are delivered to homes and businesses, cloud computing frees up businesses from having to install technology on their premises. Cloud is also known as on-demand computing, or utility computing. One version of the cloud is SaaS, or software-as-a-service (for more, see Chapter 2). In coming decades the cloud is expected to be a dominant—if not *the* dominant— mechanism for delivering computing capabilities.

ON-PREMISE SOFTWARE: The traditional way that businesses have acquired and used software: by purchasing the program—either delivered on a disc or downloaded from the Internet—and installing it on their own hardware (desktop PCs, laptops, and servers) at their physical premises. This required an upfront capital investment in both hardware and software, as well as in-house expertise to install, operate, maintain, and update the technology.

copy had to be stored in a safe place away from your office. After all, if a fire destroyed your business, you'd need to be able to retrieve copies of your important files from a place untouched by the blaze.

Backing up and storing data manually was arduous work—so arduous that many businesses simply didn't do it. Then came cloud-based remote backup. Today, businesses simply subscribe to a cloud-based backup service. For a monthly, quarterly, or annual fee, any files they designate are regularly and automatically copied and sent to a secure location over the Internet. No manual intervention needed. If a file gets corrupted for any reason, you just log on to the cloud service and download a fresh (accurate) copy. And if you're hit with a flood or fire, all your data is immediately available from a new business location.

TOP FOUR REASONS TO MOVE TO THE CLOUD

REASON 1: Reduce complexity

REASON 2: Free up time and money previously required to support technology in house

REASON 3: Get access to leading technology otherwise outside of reach

REASON 4: Add computer resources and capabilities without adding infrastructure

The History of the Cloud

As with most technology advances, the cloud didn't just appear overnight. It's been evolving for decades, and indeed represents the latest logical development in systems architecture.

In the early computing days—days of the so-called "glass house"—all processing power and data resided on a central mainframe computer. This was typically positioned inside a special air-conditioned glass enclosure in a company data center. Only technical specialists had access to these mainframes. At first, users had no direct access to these resources—they would need to make requests that were fulfilled by the technical specialists. Eventually, however, users were given "dumb" terminals—keyboards with no native intelligence built into them—that they could use to access a small subsection of the mainframe's power. All this was tightly controlled, however, and the interfaces to the applications were nongraphical and nonintuitive. (See figure 1.)

figure 1: Dumb terminals had access to the mainframe but no native intelligence built into them.

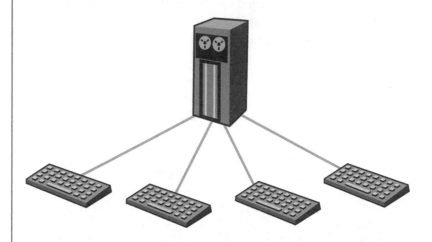

Then personal computers changed everything. At first, PCs were used as standalone devices on individual desks. Then companies began connecting them so that employees could print to a shared printer, or share files.

The next major evolution of corporate computing was client-server computing. In this phase, some of the processing power, or intelligence, of the system migrated off the mainframe (now called the server) onto the terminals (now called the clients). That is, users would be able to do some processing at their desktop PCs, even though most of the work, and most of the data, was still stored on the server. (See figure 2 on page 7.)

In many cases, client-server systems had what was called a "three-tiered" architecture: The user did some things at the PC level; most of the processing occurred at the server level, in the middle of the architecture; and the data resided on the mainframe, or the back end of the architecture.

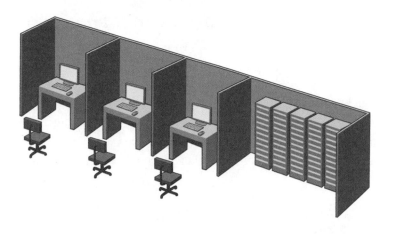

*figure 2: **With client-server computing, the data migrated off the main frame (now called the server) onto the terminals (now called the clients).***

Finally, several years after people got accustomed to having dependable, high-speed access to the Internet (dial-up access, they realized, didn't quite cut it), came the cloud. In one sense, computing has gone full circle: Users are again dependent on a remote, high-powered, and high-capacity computing resource. They don't need large, expensive, and powerful devices to access it. Everything is done—and stored—remotely, on the cloud. (See figure 3.)

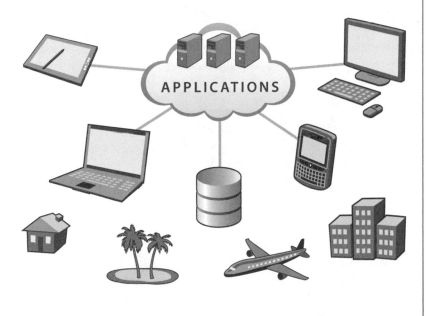

APPLICATIONS

*figure 3: **Today's view of the cloud features anytime, anywhere access from a variety of devices.***

Cloud: The Ultimate Outsourced IT Function

One way to think about cloud computing is that it enables a low-cost, no-fuss outsourcing of information technology, or IT. Just think of it: In the days of client-server computing, even a relatively small business—say, with 50 employees—needed some kind of IT expertise at hand. Even if users were fairly savvy about their desktop applications, such as word processing, spreadsheets, and databases, all employees' PCs had to be networked together

IaaS, PaaS, AND SaaS

Acronym alert! Start reading about the cloud, and you will immediately start hearing about Infrastructure as a Service (IaaS), Platform as a Service (PaaS), and Software as a Service (SaaS). What are these terms, and how do they relate to each other?

All three of these terms represent difference aspects—call them "layers"—of the cloud. This book is going to focus on SaaS. Your internal IT department (if you have one) or IT consultant (if you use an outsourced resource) might be interested in exploring IaaS or PaaS. But most of the cloud decisions you will face will involve the SaaS layer.

INFRASTRUCTURE AS A SERVICE (IAAS). You've probably heard the term *infrastructure,* but, this is an aspect of computing that is largely invisible to non IT professionals. Infrastructure is an umbrella term for all the core hardware and networking technologies that support the applications you use to run your business. This includes servers, hard drives, even the cables tying the different pieces of equipment together. It may include the operating systems, but doesn't include any "higher-level" software or data. Think of infrastructure as a house that has walls, floors, ceilings, windows, and doors, but no plumbing, electricity, or furniture. You need the infrastructure, but you can't inhabit the house without the other things.

PLATFORM AS A SERVICE (PAAS). If you subscribe to a PaaS cloud offering, you get access to the hardware and software you need to build or run business applications. In effect, PaaS is much closer to actual users than IaaS. If you extend the house metaphor, the PaaS is what makes it possible to begin using the building as a home or office. This would include the electrical wiring and the pipes, and the conduits that connect up local electric and water utilities. Once you have those things, you can begin to envision how the infrastructure can actually be useful to you.

SOFTWARE AS A SERVICE (SAAS). Finally, these are the applications that your employees actually use—such as CRM, data backup and storage, email, and so on. To stretch the house metaphor as far as it can go, when you subscribe to SaaS, you are furnishing the rooms, painting the walls, hanging the pictures, and installing the equipment and accessories that allow you to actually live or work in a space. (See *Chapter 2* for more on SaaS.)

so that they could send and receive email, exchange files, and otherwise work with one another. (The alternative was the amusingly named "Sneakernet," in which employees walked disks back and forth: data transfer by shoes.) Small business networks were notoriously unreliable—always going down, often running slowly, constantly in need of maintenance and repair. Then, if the business required any special applications—say you ran a construction company, and needed a special kind of project management database to oversee timelines, personnel, and supplies—you'd have to either purchase that specialty application or write it yourself, which in turn required having a system to store it and the data on, backing it up and storing data offsite, and troubleshooting it when it went down.

Today, with all the cloud-based applications available, *none* of this is necessary. All employees still get their own computers or laptops. But a simple wireless network gives all of them access to the Internet—which is all they need to use the numerous applications they require to do their jobs. It's the cloud service provider's job to keep things up and running. You don't worry about the costly, disruptive process of upgrading to a new version of a piece of software—it's all handled out in the cloud. Your employees may need to learn new functionality as it's made available, but you no longer have to fuss with installing or uninstalling code.

Why Businesses Love the Cloud

- **Get additional computing power and high-quality services for less cost**
  Because cloud-based service providers generally specialize in one particular function (such as email, CRM, payroll, or newsletters), they continually develop and improve the capabilities of their offerings. Since the cost is spread to many users—freeing the software provider from the costly task of having to create a version of its application for every operating system and type of hardware—the per-user price of the service may actually be less, especially when considering the cost of IT staff or consultants necessary to deploy and maintain on-premise software.

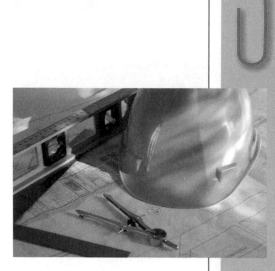

CLOUD FILE: REAL-WORLD SCENARIO

By now you may be excited, but wondering how the cloud applies specifically to your business. Consider a couple of potential scenarios showing how businesses could fully embrace the cloud:

SMALL CONSTRUCTION FIRM:

Say you run a construction company. You only have a core group of 10 employees in your office to handle such tasks as bookkeeping and payroll, HR and personnel, administrative functions, and materials purchasing. But mostly you rely on contractors. You have 60 contractors you work with regularly. At any point you may have six to 12 active projects under way, and are constantly bidding on others. In the past, processing all this activity and communicating effectively to both on-staff and contract employees would have been complicated and prone to error. But cloud computing makes your job managing all of this much easier.

For starters, you could subscribe to a cloud-based project management application. You'd give each of your contractors a username and a password for logging on to this application from wherever they happen to be—their base office, their trucks (via a smartphone or other mobile device), their home—and all of them then have complete project info at their fingertips, accurate and up-to-date, 24/7, from wherever they happen to be.

You can do payroll in the cloud as well: Your bookkeeper simply uploads the week's timesheets—submitted electronically, of course, by contractors—into the application, which calculates paychecks and withholdings, and then generates and mails checks out to contractors or pays them electronically.

You could also use a cloud-based customer relationship management (CRM) program to track new business leads and bids. Instead of having an in-house email server system that you must install and maintain, you could use an online one like Gmail from Google (with your own domain name, of course) for your company's email. And you do all this at minimal cost: 10 PCs for your in-house staff, Internet access for your office, a Wi-Fi router, and sufficient subscriptions—purchased on a per-user basis—for each of the cloud applications you use.

CHAIN OF MIDSIZE STATIONERY SHOPS:

Let's say you've got a chain of stationery stores that operate in busy malls around the country, selling high-end stationery and office supplies to both consumers and businesses. Your biggest business challenge is keeping inventory at the right level: stock too much, and you have too much money tied up in inventory; stock too little, and you risk running out and sending your customers to competitors. You choose a cloud-based inventory-management program that integrates with your cloud-based point-of-sale system, so that every time any worker in any store rings up an item for purchase, the inventory records for that particular store are adjusted accordingly. When any item's stock is reduced to a particular threshold, that store's manager is alerted and asked to approve a restock reorder.

Because this inventory management program lives in the cloud, all inventory records from all stores are automatically consolidated in a central location, and restocking orders are also consolidated before being communicated to distributors and manufacturers. This gives you bargaining power to negotiate volume discounts for the entire chain.

Such a program would have previously required a substantial upfront investment in software, along with high-priced consulting time to customize it to your chain's particular needs. Installing and configuring it at each location, and keeping the on-premise server running, would have required additional consulting time from a technology expert, since you don't keep IT staff at individual stores. However, the cloud-based inventory management service is available for a reasonable monthly fee that you count as a business expense rather than a capital expense for tax purposes. You do payroll in the cloud as well: Employees at each store log on to a cloud-based hours-tracking service, enter their hours worked each day, and the totals are processed electronically at the end of the week.

- **Get up and running quickly**
  By eliminating on-premise solutions, there's no need for you to go through the lengthy, disruptive implementation and customization processes required to deploy on-premise software. In many cases, you can be fully functional on a new product within minutes.

- **Get more predictable costs**
  Yes, you will pay a monthly, quarterly, or annual fee for cloud-based software applications, though those costs are predictable and known, unlike costs incurred when you encounter unexpected problems with your on-premise software and the hardware that hosts it.

- **Access the application and data from anywhere**
  As long as your users have Internet-capable devices and fast-enough Internet connections, they can access the applications and data from anywhere in the world. This gives businesses enormous flexibility to hire workers in various regions and create "virtual" companies that operate efficiently and cost-effectively.

- **Pay only for what you need, as you go**
  When provisioning their organizations with conventional on-premise software solutions, businesses frequently over-buy capacity to avoid the risk of not having enough. With cloud-based solutions, that rarely happens. You pay for what you use, increasing or decreasing capacity as necessary.

- **Eliminate painful software upgrades**
  Those who have been through even a minor upgrade of a mission-critical software package in their office know how disruptive that can be. With cloud-based solutions, all upgrades are seamlessly implemented by the vendor. Your users must learn the new functionality, of course. But all the pain of the upgrade itself is handled off your radar.

- **Keep your data more secure**
  Precisely because your data is all stored offsite, you don't have to worry about backing it up yourself. And it's always available, from anywhere, anytime you need it.

- **Expand your capabilities without investing in infrastructure**
  By integrating cloud solutions with your existing resources, you can add capabilities—without adding costly software or hardware.

- **Transform capital expenses to operational expenses**
  This is one of the biggest reasons so many businesses are going to the cloud: to shift the often-massive upfront investment in custom software development from a capital investment (which must be depreciated over time) to an operational expense (which can be expensed as it occurs). For any company trying to conserve cash, this is a most attractive proposition.

WHERE EXACTLY IS MY DATA?

Your data does actually have a physical location—it's not floating around out in the ether. It resides on a server "farm" in a building with an actual address—perhaps in Florida, or New York State, or South Dakota. In fact, you want to make sure your cloud service provider stores it in multiple locations. And though the storage location can change, especially for older data, your information will always have a fixed address.

checklist:

Can You Benefit from the Cloud?

Read through the questions below and check all that apply to your business.

EMPLOYEES

☐ You have trouble keeping a good IT person on staff.

☐ You can't afford to have an IT person on staff, and depend on IT consultants when something goes wrong.

☐ You want your IT person or staff to focus on higher-priority tasks or more strategic initiatives.

ACCESS

☐ You use independent contractors and external consultants and need to provide them with secure access to your systems on demand—but also must be able to turn off access at a moment's notice.

☐ You have workers in various locations—such as field sales personnel in several states, or multiple branch offices located around the world.

☐ You're always scrambling to email the latest versions of files to your team, and it seems that key documents are always stored on someone's laptop and unavailable to the team when needed.

☐ You want access to your data outside the office.

SAVINGS AND EFFICIENCY

☐ Your business needs to conserve cash.

☐ You want leading-edge software but can't afford the upfront outlay of cash.

☐ You want to leverage the equipment you already have and not buy more.

☐ You're tired of the expense and fuss involved in upgrading your on-premise software every time the vendor releases a new version, update, or patch.

☐ You don't have the time or the budget for extensively training your employees on a complex proprietary system.

☐ Although you try, you don't always back up your data every night, and you certainly don't always store it offsite.

AGILITY

☐ You have overbought computing/storage capacity because of worries that you will outgrow your existing resources.

☐ You are constantly running out of computing/storage capacity because you are growing so fast.

☐ You are uncertain how fast you will be growing, and therefore unsure how much computing capacity you will need over the next six to 12 months.

☐ You're outgrowing an existing software package, but dread the thought of either upgrading or moving to a new, on-premise one.

☐ You need software but want to get up and running now.

If you checked four or more boxes, you're a prime candidate for the cloud.

Defining Software-as-a-Service (SaaS)

By the end of this chapter...

> you'll understand what people are talking about when they say "SaaS," how SaaS applications differ from traditional "on-premise" applications, and why SaaS applications are appropriate for and beneficial to small and medium businesses."

SaaS Applications: A Vital Piece of the Cloud Story

Chapter 1 gave you a no-nonsense, plain-English definition of the cloud, along with a brief history of how it evolved. This chapter examines a specific type of cloud-based application, Software-as-a-Service (SaaS), which offers a unique set of benefits to small and medium businesses.

How is a SaaS application different from traditional software? When is a software application officially "SaaS"? This chapter outlines five character-istics that all SaaS applications have in common, so you can spot a true SaaS solution when you see one. You'll also read about the kinds of applications that are now available as SaaS services, and learn how to prioritize your SaaS needs to start planning a successful journey to the cloud.

Software-as-a-Service

There's yet another term you should add to your cloud vocabulary. That's *SaaS*, which is an acronym for Software-as-a-Service. What exactly is SaaS, and how does it relate to the cloud?

SaaS is a particular subcategory of cloud computing. It's exactly what it sounds like: software that you get in the form of a *service* rather than as a product. And that service is delivered over the Internet—the cloud—rather than being stored locally on your physical premises. You have purchased SaaS when certain functionality (which you would previously have had to buy as a piece of software and install on a computer in your office) is delivered via the cloud.

NOTE: SaaS is not the same as on-premise software that, increasingly, software companies deliver via the cloud. Although such software is designed to be installed at your business, on your own computers, you no longer have to wait for a disk to be mailed to you. Instead, you just download it from the Internet. But it's not considered SaaS if you actually have to install and run it on your own equipment.

Characteristics of SaaS Applications

Software applications that are delivered via the cloud, over the Internet—in other words, SaaS applications—share the following traits:

- **Delivered "on demand"**
  That's just what it sounds like: When you want to acquire a SaaS service, you can purchase it online at any time. Unlike on-premise software, there's no need to install it on individual users' machines. As long as your employees have Internet-capable devices and high-speed Internet connections, they're good to go.

- **Sold by subscription**
  You pay for cloud-based services as you use them. Typically, this is a flat fee based on the number of users, and is assessed monthly, quarterly, or annually. Sometimes there are different "tiers" of service—for example, certain cloud-based data backup and storage services get more expensive the more

SOFTWARE-AS-A-SERVICE (SAAS): Applications that are delivered over the Internet rather than by purchasing and installing software on your own hardware (such as servers or PCs). Both the functionality and the data "live" remotely with the cloud service provider, though some data and functionality may be downloadable for the user to access offline. SaaS (pronounced "sass") is the most common form of cloud computing in business today. This type of service is typically purchased as a subscription on a per-user basis, either monthly, quarterly, or annually.

WEB-BASED EMAIL: Email that is hosted and stored by an email provider rather than stored and managed on a company's own servers. Web-based email is generally accessible from any device, anywhere, that has an Internet connection. Popular web-based email offerings include Gmail, Microsoft Office 365, and Yahoo! Mail.

CUSTOMER RELATIONSHIP MANAGEMENT (CRM): A category of software that helps businesses retain and access data on their customers and prospects. Primarily this has been used by sales or account management teams, but CRM gives a company-wide, comprehensive view of customers, tracking interactions with them, and using up-to-the-minute information collected via a broad range of channels to improve customer service and knowledge.

SCALABILITY: The ability to add computing resources quickly, whether during peak times or in response to business growth. These resources can support an increase in the number of employees using an application, in the amount of data stored, or in the number of modules in an application that are turned on. The cloud's characteristic scalability enables companies to pay for what they use as needed and quickly add capabilities when necessary. For seasonal businesses—say, restaurants in places that see a high volume of tourists during warm months but few customers in the winter—this is a major selling point for the cloud, as they can scale up the cloud services they use when busy, and scale down when not, saving significant dollars in the process.

storage you need, while other SaaS applications offer "premium" versions with more features—but in most cases it's a consistent, rather than a variable fee that you pay on a regular basis. Different SaaS vendors offer different contracts, but in many cases if you no longer wish to use a service, you simply cancel it.

- **Scalable**
Cloud-based services can expand and contract as you need them. This is one of the cloud's biggest advantages. After all, business can be unpredictable. You may launch a new business with a small staff and suddenly see orders take off

and need to rapidly add people—and functionality. Or you may run a seasonal business that transacts 80 percent of all orders in December. Using traditional premise-based software, you would have to make expensive purchases of new hardware and software while still young and growing, or, in the second case, you'd have to significantly overbuild annual capacity—deliberately buying more technology than you needed most of the year—to avoid capacity or performance problems in December. With a cloud-based service, as your needs change, you can scale your service up or down, so you get exactly the power and capacity that you need: no more and no less.

- **Requires little or no software to download and install**
  Unlike on-premise software, where large, cumbersome computer programs needed to be installed on both servers and PC "client" machines, cloud services typically only require an Internet-capable device, a high-speed Internet connection, and a web browser loaded onto the device. Occasionally, you may need to download a driver or a small application (typically called an "app" on mobile devices). Otherwise, you're good to use your cloud-based services anywhere you can get on the Internet.

- **Flexible**
  With traditional on-premise software, all your work is stored on a company server and then is downloaded and "anchored" to a particular device (usually a specific desktop PC or laptop). If you're away from your desktop or lose your laptop (or if it's stolen), you're out of luck: no files, no spreadsheets, no databases. When you use cloud services, though, you can get at all your data, messages, and work-in-progress from any Internet-enabled device, including smartphones. You can work from anywhere in the world. And you can collaborate much more easily with colleagues, despite geographic remoteness.

What Can You Do in the Cloud?

EMAIL

One of the most widely used business functions that's moving to the cloud is email. Traditionally, most businesses hosted their own email systems: installing the software on their own hardware, and then taking responsibility for making sure it worked all the time. That meant that not only did a company have to buy email server software, it needed reliable IT personnel who could quickly respond in case there was a glitch. After all, even if your email server goes down on a night or weekend, you don't want to lose valuable messages. Not only was this expensive, it also took significant in-house technical expertise. Moreover, as people became more mobile in both their professional and their personal lives—acquiring laptops, smartphones, tablets, and other mobile devices—they needed access to these email systems from remote locations, which raised security questions as well as other technical challenges.

INTEGRATION MADE EASY

Besides adopting some of the various cloud applications available on the market today, your business can do something else quite revolutionary, quite easily, in the cloud: integrate applications together, even cloud with non-cloud-based, giving you even more capabilities and power as you run your business.

For example, you might use QuickBooks accounting software on premise. But it would be helpful to integrate some of the data you have in QuickBooks with several of the cloud-based solutions you adopt—perhaps a CRM solution, or a cloud-based marketing program such as an email newsletter program. That way, when orders are entered into QuickBooks, new customers could be automatically added to your email newsletter database, or when a salesperson closes a deal in your Salesforce CRM, an invoice could be automatically generated in QuickBooks. Using a third-party cloud *integrator* program, such as Dell Boomi, you can easily connect applications, improve your business processes, and be more productive. (For more on integration, see Chapter 9.)

Meanwhile, individuals were becoming increasingly comfortable using web-based email—such as Gmail, Microsoft's Hotmail, Yahoo! Mail, and AOL—for their personal email. They liked the flexibility of being able to access their email from anywhere. And they came to depend on the reliability of these web-based email offerings.

As a result, today, more and more businesses are switching to web-based email programs as well. Gmail, Yahoo! Mail, Microsoft's Office 365, and other brands offer web-based email for companies. Businesses get to keep their own domain names and email addresses (for example, user@mycompany.com) but they no longer have the headache of managing the back-office functions of email. The messages themselves are stored on servers belonging to the cloud email provider, and users can access their email accounts from any devices that are Internet-enabled.

Indeed, according to Osterman Research, by the end of 2011, the market for web mail will have more than doubled since 2008, when only 10 percent of all North American corporate mailboxes within midsize and large organizations were cloud-based. By the end of 2011, cloud-based email is predicted to reach 22 percent of all midsize and large email boxes.[1]

CRM

Another example of software that was traditionally delivered on premise but was one of the pioneers of SaaS is customer relationship management (CRM) software. CRM software provides tools to help businesses manage their relationships with customers. A CRM product can range from a fairly simple program that's little more than a customer contact list, to a fully integrated program that encompasses all your company's sales, marketing, and customer support functions.

For large enterprises, the traditional leading on-premise CRM software vendors were SAP and Oracle; for smaller companies, the top providers of such software were ACT!

---

1. "Why the Cloud Is Not Killing Off the On-Premises Email Market," Osterman Research, April 2011. http://ostermanresearch.com/whitepapers/download139.htm.

and Microsoft (Outlook). These companies provided massive, expensive software for sales automation and customer relations. In 1999, Marc Benioff, a former Oracle executive, founded salesforce.com—a cloud-based sales automation program that was easy enough to use and deploy and was affordable for even smaller companies. Salesforce.com took off immediately, and today it's the leader in cloud-based CRM.

In addition to CRM and email, other processes that companies are moving over to SaaS in large numbers include backup, security, storage, workflow, telephony or VoIP, accounting, payroll, marketing, and much more. For more detailed information on choosing popular types of SaaS solutions for your business, see Chapter 7 on planning your cloud strategy.

figure 1: The Salesforce Sales Executive Dashboard provides at-a-glance visibility into key sales metrics for easy daily performance monitoring.

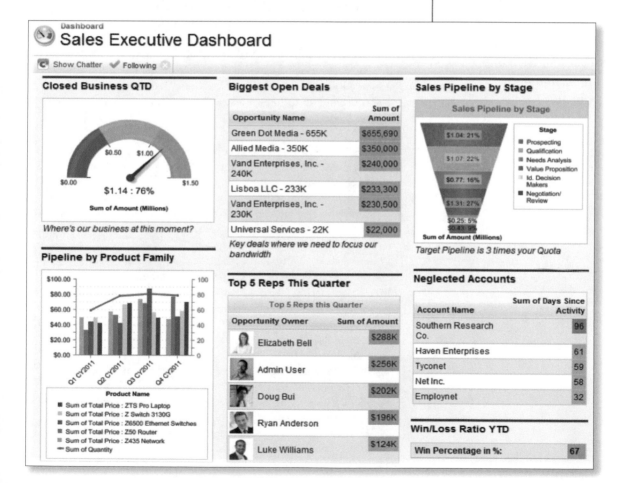

TECHSOUP
Marnie Webb, Co-CEO

"With cloud, we can make much-lighter-weight technology decisions, and take more risks," said Webb.

"We don't have to spend $35,000 and worry about whether we have made the right decision. We can try something, and if it works, we're ahead."

BACKGROUND

Founded more than 25 years ago, TechSoup is an organization with a global reach and a laser-sharp focus: to help nonprofit organizations harness technology to meet their unique missions. Itself a nonprofit, TechSoup provides technology advice, products, education, services, and support to groups ranging from small-town libraries in rural America to community healthcare clinics in Bosnia to political activists the world over. TechSoup is based in San Francisco, with 200 employees, and has offices in major cities around the globe. Its far-reaching network includes tens of thousands of volunteers, and it distributes $600 million in technology products annually to qualified nonprofits.

One of the initiatives sponsored by TechSoup is NetSquared (*www. netsquared.org*), which harnesses social media to help nonprofits improve their effectiveness in achieving their missions, motivate their bases, garner better PR and press, and have more influence on government policy. By focusing on the community-building potential of the Internet, NetSquared enables the best and brightest "technology activists" to spread the word about their ideas and innovations to promote social good on a global scale.

CHALLENGE

When she helped create NetSquared more than seven years ago, Marnie Webb, the co-CEO of TechSoup, hadn't yet heard the word *crowdsourcing*. Yet that's exactly what she was trying to do.

"We knew that nonprofits were using technology in very interesting and innovative ways," she said. "We knew that many of the problems they were individually solving were common across a broad spectrum of organizations. We wanted to tap into that."

Using Facebook, Twitter, and other social media tools, Webb and her team announced technology "challenges": competitions designed to solve problems facing many of TechSoup's core constituents. Technology activists sent in their solutions to these challenges, and the community voted on its favorites. Winners received funding or other resources to develop their ideas, and had the pleasure of seeing those ideas used on a global scale.

As the NetSquared community grew, and the projects under way multiplied, Webb realized she needed a way to manage the initiative. In particular, she wanted the NetSquared volunteers organizing face-to-face meetings in cities around the planet to be able to expand their reach. She also wanted to encourage collaboration within the local groups.

"Traditional on-premise tools wouldn't work, given the highly dispersed nature of the NetSquared network," said Webb. "The cloud clearly was the answer."

SOLUTION

Webb needed a solution—or set of solutions—that could accomplish three related but separate goals: to give local organizers a way to efficiently get the word out about upcoming meetings; to enable local groups to share their technology ideas as well as best practices on building community support in their geographic area; and to help groups manage specific agenda items that were deemed important enough to address on a global scale.

After investigating a number of cloud-based tools, Webb decided to take a "best-of-breed" approach to solutions. She settled on MeetUp to broadcast details of volunteer meetings; Google Docs for document sharing; and Basecamp for project management.

"Many cloud applications have a number of capabilities that supplement their main function," she said. "For example, we could have patched together a way to communicate our meetings using various Google products. But MeetUp had been designed specifically to do exactly what we need it to do. It even takes into account the different time zones that our meetings happen in."

BENEFITS

Today, the more than 34,000 worldwide volunteers that make up the NetSquared network organize between 70 and 80 meetings each month around the globe. Webb knows that the cloud has had a dramatic impact on NetSquared's success.

"With cloud, we can make much-lighter-weight technology decisions, and take more risks," said Webb. "We don't have to spend $35,000 and worry about whether we have made the right decision. We can try something, and if it works, we're ahead."

Webb estimates that currently 30 percent of TechSoup's applications are cloud-based, and that percentage is growing.

One reason that small businesses are moving to the cloud is simply that their employees have already done so. "You've got a choice: Deny reality or get on board," she said. Another factor driving small businesses to the cloud is the popularity of mobile consumer devices. "The cloud lets me look at the same things whether I'm at work, at home, or on the road," she said.

"I think we're going to stop talking about things like cloud and on-premise within the next three to five years," said Webb. "Everything will be interconnected and we won't be thinking about where the application or data resides, or how it comes together. And organizations will be able to do what they need to do: focus on their missions, and not on the technology that supports things." ∎

Early Adopters

Cloud-based services are rapidly being adopted by companies both large and small, and every size in between. But unlike most technology, the earliest adopters of SaaS were individuals and *smaller* businesses. Think back to the email example: Individuals used cloud-based email services (like Gmail or Yahoo! Mail) long before very many companies started migrating their email to cloud-based providers.

Once they had reliable, high-speed Internet access, individuals and small companies alike quickly saw the increases in functionality and the reduction of costs that cloud-based services offered. As a result, a whole slew of cloud-based services materialized to serve the needs of small businesses and individuals.

Who Is Moving to the Cloud?

Startups and smaller businesses, too, quickly saw the value of SaaS applications, and today new companies are among the fastest and most enthusiastic adopters of cloud-based solutions. In fact, some startups bypass traditional on-premise software altogether, such as word processing and spreadsheet programs, in favor of cloud-based SaaS solutions such as Google Docs. It makes good sense. Startups are usually strapped for cash. Using cloud-based solutions, they don't have to cover the large capital expenses in software or more powerful hardware. Instead, they get a monthly operating expense—an attractive proposition indeed. The flexibility that SaaS solutions offer to a new business is also attractive. If a particular SaaS solution turns out to be wrong for the business, it can quickly change—there are no sunk costs to prevent switching.

SaaS and On-Premise Solutions: Examples

TYPE OF SOFTWARE/ SOLUTION	ON-PREMISE PRODUCTS EXAMPLES	SAAS/CLOUD PRODUCTS EXAMPLES
Email	Microsoft Exchange Server Microsoft Outlook IBM Lotus Notes	Gmail Microsoft Hotmail Yahoo! Mail
Customer relationship management (CRM)	Oracle CRM SAP CRM	Salesforce CRM SugarCRM Zoho CRM
Data backup and storage	NOVAbackup DT Utilities PC Backup Genie Backup Manager	Dropbox iBackup Norton Online Backup
Marketing/ newsletters	Email Marketing Director SendBlaster Atomic Mail Sender	Marketo Eloqua Constant Contact Vertical Response
Project management	Oracle Primavera P6 Microsoft Project @Task	Genius Project Daptiv Projecturf PBworks Basecamp
Time-tracking and billing	Atlantic Global Metratech	Timesheet.com Pacific Timesheet
Customer support/ communities	*Virtually all on-premise customer support applications for small and medium businesses have moved to the cloud or are a combination of on-premise and cloud*	Get satisfaction.com ZenDesk Lithium Jive

CLOUD FILE: REAL-WORLD SCENARIO

SMALL VETERINARY OFFICE:

A small veterinary office mailed out a quarterly printed newsletter to its clients, offering tips on how to keep their pets healthy. After all, newsletters are a great way to keep a company's name in front of customers. However, it was costly and time-consuming to prepare a physical mailing and maintain and manage a mailing list. The vet's office wanted to change to an email newsletter, but didn't have the resources or capability to install and manage mailing software, continually clean up the mailing list, and lay out the graphics and the content. Then cloud-based email providers like Constant Contact, Vertical Response, and others came along providing simple templates and automated mailing list management for a predictable and low monthly fee. Suddenly, the vet's administrative assistant could manage the entire process in a fraction of the time it would take to prepare a print mailing. The cloud solution enabled the vet's office to increase newsletter frequency to every month, and save money at the same time.

worksheet:

Your Business Priorities

Use this worksheet to determine what types of cloud applications interest you, to take an inventory of what you currently use, and to prioritize the importance of implementing the applications.

TYPE OF CLOUD-BASED SOLUTION	CURRENT SOLUTION (IF ANY)	PRIORITY (HIGH, MEDIUM, LOW)
Email		
Customer relationship management (CRM)		
Data backup and storage		
Marketing/newsletters		
Project management		
Time-tracking and billing		
Customer support/ communities		
Inventory management		
Accounting		
Human resources		
Other:		

No doubt when you read about the cloud, you will run into terms like virtualization and public or private clouds. Here's what they mean:

VIRTUALIZATION: In computing, virtualization is to make a "virtual" copy of something that acts like the real thing. It usually refers to hardware. You can virtualize hardware in two different ways.

First, you can divide up a single physical machine into multiple "virtual" machines, each of which can run a separate operating system as well as other applications and software. In effect, you are turning one PC or server into two, or five, or 10 unique PCs or servers. Why would you do this? To get the most out of the hardware you've purchased.

For example, say you use some software in your business that runs under Microsoft Windows, and some that runs under the UNIX operating system. Without virtualization, you would have to buy two different machines to run these two different types of applications. If you use virtualization to create two virtual machines, you can run all your software on a single PC.

You can also use virtualization to do the opposite: to combine many different machines so that they operate as a single machine. You would want to do this if you have an application that outgrows the capacity of one PC, for example. Rather than having to abandon that PC and buy a bigger one, you can simply take another PC, and use that to extend the capacity of the original one.

PUBLIC CLOUD VS. PRIVATE CLOUD: You may hear a particular cloud described as "public" or "private." Here are the differences:

PUBLIC CLOUD: When you hear the term "cloud" it generally refers to the public cloud, where applications or other services are delivered to a broad range of people or businesses over the Internet. This book focuses on public clouds.

PRIVATE CLOUD: A private cloud is a cloud that is used by a single organization. Sometimes large businesses build their own private clouds for security or cost reasons, although the large economies of scale that generally make cloud computing attractive can be difficult to achieve with a private cloud.

Silver Linings: Benefits of the Cloud

By the end of this chapter...

you'll understand the benefits associated with using SaaS, and start to plan which processes or departments at your company would most benefit from adopting cloud applications.

Why Move to the Cloud?

Every cloud has a silver lining, and cloud-based applications have many. This chapter outlines some of the more compelling issues that are motivating businesses to move to the cloud. Money is a big factor of course, and cloud solutions help you both save it and make more of it. But in addition, when you adopt SaaS applications, you can also expect process improvements such as mobile productivity and team collaboration. And then there's the increased business insight for the management team, with tools like real-time alerts.

From greater functionality to plain old ease-of-use, there are numerous good reasons why so many businesses, both large and small, are choosing cloud-based applications over on-premise solutions.

learn the lingo

Financial Rewards

Money is clearly one of the biggest factors behind the business push to the cloud. It's no coincidence that the popularity of cloud-based applications began to mushroom around the same time that the worldwide economy slumped. That's because the cloud provides many financial advantages when a company seeks to acquire the technology resources it needs to prosper in difficult times.

With the cloud, there are financial tradeoffs—for some companies, the lifetime cost of a cloud-based application may actually be greater than the upfront costs of purchasing an on-premise application—but there are many obvious financial benefits.

- **Upfront capital investment**
  When you start with a cloud-based application rather than an on-premise one, you don't need to invest large amounts of cash in software programs and the hardware necessary to run them. This is a considerable advantage for an expanding or new company, or for one looking for a different software solution. Additionally, when it's time in an existing company to upgrade from a current on-premise software application, doing so can be a huge capital expense. Moving applications to the cloud avoids the big financial hit of a company-wide upgrade.

- **Favorable tax treatment**

  The cost of cloud-based solutions also carries with it what most companies consider a tax benefit. Rather than having to account for the costs of software as capital expenses and thus depreciate those expenses over time, cloud subscriptions are treated as an operational expense. This means that the full cost of the application subscription can be deducted every year, rather than over a number of years. This is generally beneficial.

- **Predictable costs**

  Many businesses appreciate the predictability of cloud-based solutions. You pay a fixed fee each month, quarter, or year (of course, more if you add users and capacity, less if you subtract them). If and when something goes wrong with a cloud solution, you don't have the unexpected costs of having to fix it—that is, the variable expenses of IT personnel and consultants. All this makes cash flow easier to manage.

- **Reduced hardware and other infrastructure costs**

  Cloud-based solutions require fewer and less powerful computing resources onsite. When you adopt cloud applications, you eliminate the need both for the servers that host the applications and data and for physical office space that those servers require. And when you need to expand your cloud-based systems, you simply move up to the next tier of service rather than expand your onsite infrastructure. You'll also prolong the life of the computers you already have. Since your cloud-based applications don't require a great deal of local processing power, but only a high-speed Internet connection, you can work just fine with less powerful and less expensive computers.

  With cloud applications you save money in other ways. For one, you won't overbuy capacity and functionality, since in the cloud you choose—and pay for—only the level of functionality you want. You also eliminate the risk of making costly purchasing mistakes. Say you buy an on-premise software application but soon realize your employees dislike it. High switching costs mean you're likely stuck with it for a while.

factoid

"Mr. Watson—come here—I want to see you." So spoke Alexander Graham Bell in 1876 to his assistant through his new device, the telephone. Sixteen years later, in 1892, AT&T built a long-distance line between New York City and Chicago. It could handle one call at a time at a cost of $9 for the first five minutes. By 1927, transatlantic calls were possible—at a cost of $75 for the first three minutes. Today? With the cloud-based VoIP darling Skype, you can place a "call" from your computer to the computer of any other Skype user in the world—for free. (And if he had a webcam, Alexander Graham Bell could now actually "see" Mr. Watson for free, too.)

And during that time, your business can suffer due to lost worker productivity.

In addition, staying current with your on-premise software can require expensive upgrades. You have to ensure that everyone on your team has the same version, of course. And when you do upgrade your software—and sometimes you'll have to upgrade the hardware as well—you're likely to suffer inconvenient downtime. An underlying assumption is that you'll need IT professionals to install and maintain your software over its lifetime. You may also need to pay external training companies to get your employees up to speed on the software functionality.

With the cloud, many of these expenses simply disappear. Switching providers is less painful because you have invested much less money and time upfront. You'll also always have the latest version, since the cloud vendor takes responsibility for upgrading the solution, resulting in little, if any, downtime for you. Plus, any technical problems belong to the cloud vendor. You end up spending far less time on IT support and trouble-shooting and more time innovating.

Functionality, Efficiency, and Innovation

Although money is a great motivator for adopting cloud solutions, many other benefits come from the cloud.

One of the more powerful benefits the cloud offers is increased efficiency from spending less time learning, installing, and maintaining programs, and more time doing your job.

- **Greater innovation**
  Most cloud-based applications are continually being enhanced. Cloud providers don't have to wait to incorporate new features in the next upgrade. Instead, they can make continuous incremental improvements. Also, cloud-based applications give growing businesses access to computing resources and capabilities at a much lower price point than traditional applications. Even the smallest companies get the kind of functionality previously only available to the largest corporations. With the playing field leveled in this way, smaller businesses run far more efficiently, and can compete more effectively with larger enterprises.

HOW CAN CUTTING-EDGE FUNCTIONALITY ACTUALLY COST LESS?

One reason cloud applications are so economical is that the software service provider has many customers—or tenants—using the software residing on its servers. In effect, the cloud application provider has developed a centralized, consolidated solution that thousands of customers use. These customers share the costs, reducing them for all participants. This is comparable to erecting an apartment complex rather than many separate houses—each unit costs less to build and service, and expenses are shared, so costs are naturally lower. And an application that an individual business may use only for a few hours a day is utilized 24/7 in the cloud because of users distributed around the globe.

Another reason that cloud prices are lower than on-premise solutions is due to the efficiency of the business model. Traditional on-premise software depends on creating, marketing, and selling upgrades every year or two. Distribution costs and software piracy also eat into software manufacturers' profits. All of this makes the revenue stream unpredictable. With a subscription-based cloud service, revenues are steady. Piracy is eliminated, and upgrades can be pushed out continuously. All these efficiencies result in lower cost for the customer.

Yet one more reason that cloud-based applications can be less expensive is that the software provider doesn't have to develop and maintain multiple versions of its program to serve different operating systems and OS versions. With on-premise software, a software provider might need to develop and support two or three versions of Microsoft Windows, for example (such as Windows 7, Vista, and XP) as well as versions of OS X for Apple computers, along with mobile platforms such as Android, iOS, and Windows mobile. But with a cloud-based application, users access the software through a web browser, eliminating the problem of operating system compatibility and cutting the developers' costs. Supporting multiple browsers is far easier and cheaper than supporting multiple operating systems.

- **Improved response time**
  The speed of deployment of cloud applications means businesses can be up and running with a new application within days or even hours rather than weeks or months when a new market opportunity opens up. This increased agility makes businesses far more competitive. Projects get off the ground faster, as cloud-based applications help you automate key business processes and make decisions in real time. Expanding your workforce becomes easier, too, when you can provide new employees (or contractors) with full software capabilities within minutes.

- **Greater ease-of-use**
Cloud-based applications are frequently designed to be easy to learn and use quickly. This means your employees will require minimal training to get up and running with the new product. It's less frustrating for them and more productive for you, the business manager. So that top-notch sales team can hit the pavement and be immediately productive rather than wasting time learning how to use complicated software. What training your team does need is typically also delivered on-demand via online videos and webinars that let employees learn quickly in their own way, at their own pace. This is a vast improvement over the old way of doing things, which typically involved flying to a remote location for a week of training.

- **Collaboration**
The cloud also makes collaboration far easier, which increases productivity. Multiple users can share data and files. You can collaborate in real time with someone halfway around the globe or down the hall. Contrast that with emailing a document back and forth, editing it, saving it, renaming it, and emailing it around again for final approvals—all of which makes your Inbox unmanageable and documents difficult and time-consuming to find. Collaboration is one of the cloud's best benefits.

- **Anytime/anywhere access**
Because your data is stored over the Internet on providers' servers and accessed via a web browser, all designated members of your team can work anytime, virtually anywhere, as long as they have high-speed Internet access. Since cloud applications function independently of specific hardware, increasingly your employees will be able to work on tablets, smartphones, or other devices in addition to laptops and desktop computers. This allows them to work in the office, from home, in a hotel room, at a trade show, or at the airport. Anywhere there's an Internet connection, your employees

1. "A Computer Wanted," *The New York Times*, May 2, 1892, http://query.nytimes.com/mem/archive-free/pdf?res=9F07E0D81438E233A25751C0A9639C94639ED7CF.

can be productive. And anytime you visit vendors or customers, you—or authorized members of your team—have crucial company information at your fingertips.

The cloud also enables managers to stay in touch with their teams while on the road. They can track the progress of deals, approve new customer credit applications, and speed up fulfillment by managing inventory from anywhere around the globe.

- **Integrated data**
  With the new cloud integration tools, you will be able to share information across a broad range of applications—and not just your cloud-based applications, but your traditional, on-premise software programs as well. You enter data just once and it flows across all affected applications, including sales, marketing, customer services, accounting, human resources, and audits. You save money with this type of tight integration: no more reentering duplicate information in conflicting programs, no more troubleshooting the results of data entry errors that cause misalignment of reports that should be in sync. (See Chapter 9 for more on integration.)

BUSINESS INFORMATION YOU NEED ACCESS TO

- Account files
- Accounting records
- Current or backed-up files
- Customer contact information
- Human resource files
- Intellectual property
- Marketing campaigns
- Project management
- Sales leads

Management Control

One rarely discussed positive aspect of adopting cloud computing is that it gives managers much more insight into how their businesses are actually operating, while at the same time keeping company data secure. This is vital for both short-term competitiveness and long-term survival.

- **Greater business visibility and transparency**
Cloud-based applications enable managers to better monitor—and manage—what's going on in the company. Because the data is stored on the web and shared with all designated employees, a manager can access information that used to reside solely on individual employees' desktops or deep within company files stored on servers. Cloud-based applications typically make it easier to extract the right data as well. Want to know if your salesperson closed that big deal? Just log on to your cloud-based CRM application and check it out for yourself. Or, even better, set an auto "alert" that triggers an email or text to you when a deal closes. That way, you'll never be uncertain whether a particular customer shipment went out on time. When it does, the proof is in the cloud.

GAIN A COMPETITIVE EDGE WITH ANALYTICS

One of the most overlooked—and greatest—competitive advantages of the cloud is its analytics capability. (See Chapter 10 for more on this.) Today, it's likely that you've had to assign one or more employees to be responsible for merging data they've extracted from different systems into specially designed Excel spreadsheets. The problem is, too many things can "break" in this process. What if your analytics specialists are sick, or quit? Chances are good they're the only ones who really understand where the data is, how to extract it, and how the spreadsheet works. With cloud-based analytics, all your users can gain easy access to data in one place that enables them to spot trends, look for new opportunities, and get a jump on the competition.

worksheet:

How Much Time Does Your Team Spend on Core Activities?

A great benefit of the cloud is that it frees up your team to focus on core activities. Fill out this worksheet to estimate how much time your staff spends on core activities versus noncore activities. Remember to include other core or noncore activities not listed here.

STAFF	CORE ACTIVITIES	TIME SPENT/ MONTH ON CORE ACTIVITIES (HRS/WEEK)	NONCORE ACTIVITIES REDUCED/ELIMINATED BY CLOUD SOLUTIONS	TIME SPENT/ MONTH ON NONCORE ACTIVITIES (HRS/WEEK)
IT	Innovation		Support, maintenance, performing custom calculations/ analytics/data retrieval on demand for business users	
Accounting	Forecasting expenses and revenues; finding cost reductions; financial analysis		Data entry; generating reports at user requests	
Marketing	Analyzing data to create and launch effective marketing campaigns; analyzing campaigns' effectiveness; creating marketing campaigns and materials		Preparing contact lists for campaigns; cleansing lists of duplicates/errors; entering results of marketing campaigns into spreadsheets and analytics programs	
Business Intelligence	Analyzing data: looking for trends, opportunities, threats, and changes in business conditions; identifying key drivers of success		Organizing and preparing data for analysis	
Sales	Making sales calls; closing deals; finding and following up on leads; getting deals approved		Searching for data; preparing sales reports; waiting for approval on deals	
Other:				

WINTER SKI RESORT:

Seasonal businesses can benefit greatly from the cloud's flexibility. Take a ski resort. Winters are clearly their high season, summers the low. But some winters have more snow and therefore a longer season than others. There's no precise way to predict the timing of the changeover from one season's activities to the next. By using the cloud to do payroll, manage inventory, and handle bookings, management can quickly scale up in winter, when the employee head count at resorts is highest (ski instructors, groomers, lift operators, ski patrol and hotel, retail, and wait staff). When the skiing season is over, the resort can then scale down to support summer tourism activities. The resort pays only for the services it needs, when it needs them. For a seasonal business with widely fluctuating cash flow based on variable weather conditions, aligning costs to revenues is key to success.

- **Secures company assets**
  Right now, it's likely that many critical company documents are sitting on the desks (or in the paper files) of many of your employees. What happens if a star salesperson decides to leave? The contact list and status of pending deals may walk out the door, too. How about the details of an urgent project if a key employee is taken ill? Instead of having to search through a sick worker's PC for the Excel file tracking deliverables, you can just go to the cloud.

- **Real-time alerts in a dynamic business environment**
  Thanks to the combination of integration, real-time data access, and analytics, you know when you're near critical business thresholds. For example, a cloud-based CRM service can notify your VP of sales if revenue drops below a certain threshold. Or you know when customer demographics shift or inventory levels get dangerously high in your Enterprise Resource Planning (ERP) system (see page 30 for a definition of ERP). Best of all, you can customize alerts and

reports to meet your specific needs. For example, you can set alerts so that you are notified by email or text when a member of your team has updated an important document.

- **Backup and disaster recovery**
Earthquakes, tornadoes, floods, storms, and other emergencies happen. But if your data is stored in the cloud you'll always have access to it, and you'll be able to restart your business faster. In a major disaster, you'll be able to receive insurance or federal funds much more quickly if you can retrieve your critical records and data such as financials, customer files, legal records, and intellectual property. And if a disaster forces your employees to work from a different location than your main place of business, they'll still be able to log on to their cloud-based applications and retrieve data anytime, anywhere.

THE BEAUTY OF INTEGRATION: COST-PER-CALL REPORT EXAMPLE

When key data lives in separate applications, a task that should be simple, like generating a call-per-cost report, involves several steps:

Step 1: Pull call data from the CRM database.

Step 2: Go to your finance application, navigate to the right record, and pull revenue information.

Step 3: Do computations and generate graphs in Excel.

This process is labor intensive, time consuming, and error prone—and therefore not done as often as desired. But, when applications are "integrated" and set up to share data with each other, all of that can happen automatically. Even add a third application: payroll. Then you can factor in compensation data to assess not just cost per call, but revenue by sales rep as well.

With integrated applications, sales performance metrics are easier to evaluate on a regular basis.

Cloud Benefits-at-a-Glance

TRADITIONAL ON-PREMISE SOFTWARE	CLOUD-BASED SOFTWARE
Large initial investment of capital for an asset that is depreciated over time	Predictable, monthly fee that can be written off as an operating expense
Unpredictable, variable costs (e.g., IT support, upgrades, add-ons) and ongoing licensing fees	Fixed, monthly, pay-as-you-go costs
Expensive and time-consuming upgrades that lead to versioning problems	All users are always on the same, most up-to-date version
High costs to switch to a different solution	Relatively easy to move to a more appropriate cloud alternative
Pay for functionality you may neither need nor want	Pay only for what you need
Adding users, storage capacity, or add-on features can be costly and time consuming	Simple to add more users or resources as needed
Need to invest in additional hardware infrastructure to expand capabilities	Add capabilities with no incremental hardware expenses. If you are adding users, you just need to give a Web browser–capable device to each new user; if you want to add capabilities to the application itself, you simply configure your cloud service to add the new functions. No need to install new software on each and every user's computer
Requires time and attention by IT professionals to support and maintain	Cloud vendor takes responsibility for support and maintenance of application, as well as for the hardware it runs on, the backup of all data, and its connectivity to the Internet
User tied to desktop	Anytime access from any device with Internet access enables a globally productive team
Requires weeks or months of implementation time	Immediate availability
Requires regular backups to keep data safe	Data is always secure and available in an offsite location
Data always lags behind the business, impeding insight and collaboration	Data and analytics are always fresh and available in real time, enabling easy collaboration
Individual employees can hoard information and take it with them when they leave the organization	Company assets such as operational and customer data and other intellectual property (IP) stays with the firm even if employees leave
Training can be time consuming and costly	Easy to learn and use, so employees can focus on the business

4

Showers Ahead? Concerns about the Cloud

By the end of this chapter...

you'll have learned about some of the drawbacks and vulnerabilities of the cloud. You'll know what issues you need to address to make the cloud work for you, and what questions to ask cloud service providers before signing a contract.

An Ounce of Prevention...

Chapter 3 was devoted to the many benefits of cloud applications for growing businesses. They're very real. But it's also important for you to understand some of the concerns relating to this new technology platform as you plan your transition to the cloud.

Security concerns are often top-of-mind when cloud solutions are being explored. While we touch on that subject here, Chapter 5 is devoted exclusively to the subject of privacy and security in the cloud. In this chapter, we'll consider other could-be gotcha's—things like vendor reliability, remote data access, and employee resistance—that you'll want to address before you proceed.

With a realistic understanding of the concerns, you'll be better prepared to ask the right questions of service providers, troubleshoot issues in advance, and get the most from your cloud-based services.

Privacy and Security Risks

The number one concern businesses express when considering moving to the cloud are issues of security and privacy: Will my data be there when I want it, and will it be safe from unauthorized users? These are such critical issues that an entire chapter is devoted to them (see Chapter 5).

Even the top security firms scramble to keep abreast of the latest malware, viruses, spyware, and other things that can damage or corrupt systems or data, or violate employees' or customers' privacy. Of course, these risks aren't limited to cloud applications. Any business with systems that are connected to the outside world—which naturally includes on-premise software as well as cloud applications—is vulnerable.

It's essential to look at the privacy and security dangers that are unique to the cloud. Your data is no longer stored on your hardware on your business premises. You have much less control over its safety. You must depend on whatever protective measures the vendor has put into place. Cloud applications are specifically designed to enable easy access to them from anywhere in the world. Does that make them easier to break into than on-premise software? Some experts argue that might be the case; others argue it makes them safer.

Among other things, Chapter 5 provides an extensive checklist of questions you should ask a potential cloud vendor about privacy and security. This is a critical step in vetting the vendors that are truly trustworthy.

Access

Will your employees be able to work whenever they need to? Their reliance on applications that live on the Internet adds another critical component to your working environment. Cloud applications require you to have reliable, high-speed Internet access. That's nonnegotiable. If you can't connect to the web, you can't log on to your SaaS payroll, CRM, ERP application, or any other application. Nor can you access the data stored in those applications. If you have important work to do that requires access to these applications—and the more you operate in the cloud, the more you will—you are in trouble

1. "It's cloud prediction time: IDC, Gartner (and I) weigh in," by Derrick Harris, December 1, 2011, GigaOM. http://gigaom.com/cloud/its-cloud-prediction-time-idc-gartner-and-i-weigh-in/.

UPTIME: Typically expressed as a percentage, uptime is the amount of time the cloud-based service is available for use. The gold standard for uptime is 99.999 percent.

CONFIGURABLE: The ability to choose how to align software to your business needs, culture, and processes. Most cloud-based programs are easily configurable. You simply choose from a menu of options the ones that suit your business best.

CUSTOMIZABLE: Tailor-made applications that are developed for a particular company's unique needs. Typically, these types kinds applications require expert help to develop and maintain them.

SERVICE LEVEL AGREEMENT (SLA): The part of a business contract for services, such as delivering a cloud application, where the quality of service is defined. Typically, the definition includes quantitative measures, such as percentage of uptime, mean time between failures (MTBF), or mean time to recovery (MTTR).

whenever the Internet is not available. This challenge is for you to solve, since the cloud application provider has no control over this. For example, if your workers frequently travel in China or Australia, you should be aware that the "pipes" there that convey web traffic are small and unreliable. You may well have problems deploying a mission-critical SaaS application if your users need to access it in either region. Also, some cloud applications—even specific features within a cloud application—require greater capacity than others. If you need to do a lot of complex calculations using a cloud application that pulls information from many different sources, that could suffer from a poor Internet connection.

Given that most small businesses now have reliable high-speed Internet access, the access issue at the workplace is whether your Internet access is consistently running with no significant interruptions. For most businesses, especially in developed economies, it is. But if your workers are viewing a lot of streaming videos or listening to music over the web, that can slow down everything you're doing in the cloud at your place of business. If you are thinking of moving a highly critical business function to the cloud, you might consider hiring a consultant to analyze what types of web "traffic" your business generates, how much of it, and when it's busiest, to identify whether you're taking any risks with a cloud application.

The question of Internet access becomes even more urgent when employees work from places other than the main office. Most mobile employees have laptops as well as smartphones and even tablets equipped with Wi-Fi capabilities. Since Wi-Fi is available in most business hotels, airports and other transportation hubs, and many other public places, this is less of a problem than it used to be. But even major business hotels in New York City can have Internet connectivity problems, since public Wi-Fi connections are often slow due to heavy traffic. In this case, you may not be able to access all your data all the time.

Luckily, you have some workarounds. For example, you may be able to keep working if your cloud application allows you to easily download data to your own device and work "offline." Likewise, USB modems on cell phones can be used to access cloud applications if cellular service is available. However, it's a fact that with cloud-based applications, your ability to be productive, and the ability of your employees to do their work, depends primarily on your ability to get online. If your mobile employees will typically be operating in places where high-speed Internet access is likely to be unavailable or unreliable, you'll have access problems that need to be addressed when you consider whether to move to the cloud and which providers to use.

Reliability

This question of *access* has another angle: How reliable is the cloud-based application or service provider you're considering? That is, can you trust that the vendor can keep its service operational around the clock, 365 days a year?

After all—as all businesses are painfully aware—systems go down. Their own on-premise hardware breaks down, their internal networks fail, their on-premise software has glitches that foul up their ability to use it. The same problems have the potential to plague cloud-based applications.

When major cloud applications that serve millions of users worldwide go down, it's headline news with serious consequences for the businesses that depend on them. Even cloud

worksheet:

Questions to Ask Yourself about Access Requirements

Answer the following questions to help determine what kind of access you require to an application you are considering for the cloud.

Application: _____

1. Are the employees who need to use this cloud application highly mobile?

    _____

2. What percentage of the time will the affected employees need high-speed Internet access?

    _____

3. What percentage of the time will the affected employees not have high-speed Internet access?

    _____

4. How critical is the cloud application for letting these employees do their jobs?

    _____

5. How critical is it to your business that these employees be able to access the cloud application when they need to?

    _____

6. What functions and data can be handled on employees' hard drives in the event they can't access the Internet?

    _____

    _____

7. What's your "Plan B" should employees not be able to log on to the cloud application when required? (For example, will they need to telephone someone in the company to extract the information or input the data for them?)

    _____

    _____

    _____

    _____

    _____

    _____

SERVICE LEVEL AGREEMENT (SLA)

A *service level agreement*, or SLA, is an essential part of any contract you sign with a cloud vendor. It documents the quality of service that the vendor promises to deliver to you. SLAs are common in business and used in a broad range of industries. Any contract that has a service component will typically include an SLA. In SLAs for cloud services, note two critical points: The first is the guaranteed uptime, expressed as a percentage: 99 percent; 99.5 percent; 99.9 percent; 99.99 percent; and so on. The second is the financial penalty that the vendor will pay to you if the SLA is not met. Penalties tend to be higher for more mission-critical—and more costly—applications. If your business would be severely affected or disrupted by a SaaS application or other cloud service going down, you should negotiate for the highest SLA, and demand the most severe penalty if that SLA is violated.

heavyweights have had their embarrassing moments when their systems were inaccessible for hundreds of thousands, even millions, of users. Generally, these outages don't last long, but they do happen, and they could happen when you need to perform a critical business function.

Two lessons can be learned here. First, understand that no cloud vendor is infallible. So go into the cloud with eyes wide open, understanding that sooner or later you may be inconvenienced by technical problems of your cloud vendor, just as sooner or later you're likely to be inconvenienced by crashes or glitches with your on-premises hardware or software. Of course, when your own on-premises technology goes down, not only do you have an interruption, it's *your* problem. And you must assume the headache and costs of solving it. By contrast, when a cloud application goes down, the problem is someone else's to fix.

The second lesson is, reduce your risk as much as possible by researching your cloud vendor. Before you sign any cloud contract, thoroughly research the vendor (see worksheet, page 47). Choose vendors that have a reputation for quality and responsiveness and that you trust will work to ensure the fewest possible interruptions and have the capabilities to provide consistent reliability.

Make sure you find out a vendor's promised *uptime*—typically expressed as a percentage. For example, 99 percent uptime means the service is available 99 percent of the time. Is that going to be good enough for you? Probably not.

worksheet:

How to Research Vendor Reliability

To research a potential vendor, go through the steps below and make notes on the information you find.

Vendor: _____

1.   Review the vendor's standard SLA.

   _____

   _____

   _____

2.   How successful has the vendor been at meeting this SLA with existing customers?

   _____

   _____

   _____

3.   If you're not comfortable with the standard SLA—if you are considering a cloud application that is truly mission-critical to your business—inquire whether you can pay for a premium SLA.

   _____

   _____

   _____

4.   Ask for references (always), and actually call them and talk to them.

   _____

   _____

   _____

5.   Do a thorough Internet search on the vendor. Search terms to use: *vendor name, uptime, crash, downtime, reliability, complaints, problems, SLA penalties.*

   _____

   _____

   _____

   _____

The gold standard for uptime is what's called "Five 9's," or 99.999. Your vendor may not be able to promise that—or you may have to pay more for a service-level agreement (SLA) (see SLA sidebar, page 46) that guarantees that. But make sure you ask.

NOTE: All these measures refer to unscheduled *downtime. Your cloud vendor will inevitably have periods when it must take the application down to perform maintenance or upgrades. In such cases, however, you typically receive plenty of advance notice so you can plan accordingly.*

Ways to Measure SLAs

TYPE OF MEASURE	DEFINITION
Percentage of uptime	Percentage of time application is available
Mean time between failures (MTBF)	The average time the application stays "up" between crashes
Mean time to recovery (MTTR)	The average time it takes for a vendor to make a cloud application available to users after a failure

Customization

Can you get an "off-the-shelf" cloud-based application to meet your specific needs? Will it work to do the things you absolutely must do?

Although the cloud business applications coming onto the market are increasingly *configurable*, they tend to be less *customizable* than on-premise applications. What's the difference? With a configurable SaaS application, you typically have a number of choices for how to set it up that help you align the application to your business needs, culture, and processes. These choices are usually very easily made through drop-down menus or dashboards or "toggle" buttons, and you can make choices that affect all users within your business, or allow users to make their own individual choices.

As cloud applications become more sophisticated, the more closely you can tailor them to your needs. But, generally, there's a limit to the number of choices vendors provide, for two reasons. First is cost: The vendor will invest in developing configurability options based on the needs of the overall market. There is inevitably a point of diminishing returns for offering more choices that only a few customers are interested in. Second is ease of use: The more complex the application, the more difficult it is to use. Adding too many optional bells and whistles can actually make a cloud application less attractive to businesses because it is more difficult to get employees up to speed.

INDUSTRY-SPECIFIC SOFTWARE: FINALLY ENTERING THE CLOUD

Most early cloud applications were designed to appeal to general business audiences, and included general payroll and accounting, collaboration, CRM, ERP, and HR solutions. Yet many small businesses rely on software that was built for the unique requirements of their specific industry. For example, there is specialized accounting software to support businesses that import goods from Asia; purchasing software specifically designed for construction companies that remodel homes; and point-of-sale software for retailers that sell clothes and fashion accessories. Until fairly recently, this industry-specific software was primarily available only in on-premise versions. That's changing. Today, certain cloud-based solutions target individual industries, even highly niched ones. For example, the New York Stock Exchange (NYSE) offers a cloud solution for financial services companies looking for a secure online service that gives them immediate access to NYSE market data, and which allows them to store data and develop their own internal cloud applications. There's a life sciences cloud solution to help pharmaceutical and medical device companies track all gifts to physicians, including cash, entertainment, travel, meals, and funding for research. It's likely that there's a cloud-based solution for *your* industry. Or soon will be.

Keep in mind, though, that certain cloud vendors have evolved their applications to the point where they're much more than simply applications—they're what the computer industry calls *platforms.* Salesforce.com is an example of this, with its AppExchange and Force.com. The application has become so popular that an entire ecosystem has grown up around it. You can easily find other cloud applications that have been designed to extend the usefulness of the basic salesforce.com service, as well as expert consultants who can make it do virtually anything you need (see ISYS case study, page 130). In fact, the "sales" in salesforce.com is really a misnomer at this point, since the platform can be customized to fit any number of other business needs, or to address concerns that are unique to individual industries, like healthcare, retail, or manufacturing operations.

For these reasons, most cloud applications can't compete with highly customized or customizable on-premise applications that you have had built or can tailor to meet your business's unique needs. But, those customizable applications typically require highly expert help to actually *do* the customizing and the ongoing maintenance. They can take a long time to install. All this adds up to a much higher cost than cloud-based solutions. But if your business has a unique way of doing things—and those methods are truly mission-critical—you may find that cloud applications aren't a good fit, regardless of how much money and time you save and ease-of-use you gain by going to the cloud.

Of course, if you're already using off-the-shelf solutions—software that you've minimally tweaked, if at all—then you're likely to find cloud-based solutions that offer the same, if not greater, functionality and ability to configure.

Variable Performance

Concerns about performance have long topped the list of cloud naysayers. And for legitimate reasons. Few things are more frustrating for business users than being forced to wait for a response from a system. That was true with on-premise software—whether due to slow hardware or to an overloaded internal network—and it's true with cloud applications.

The problem lies in the number of variables that affect how a SaaS application or cloud service performs. Think about it: Your laptop or smartphone might be old, or need an upgrade. Your Internet connection could be poor. The global Internet itself might be running sluggishly at any given time because of a broad range of factors. The cloud vendor's hardware could be at fault. Or there could simply be too many users on that particular cloud application at once, and all users are affected.

The good news is that *all* these factors will only improve over time, as the overall global Internet infrastructure is continually strengthened, technical and communications innovations proliferate, and cloud vendors build on their existing knowledge

---

2. "Salesforce.com Announces Fiscal Third Quarter Results," November 17, 2011. http://www.salesforce.com/ company/news-press/press-releases/ 2011/11/111117.jsp.

and expertise. The bad news is that the nature of the cloud model gives you, in fact, little control over the performance of your cloud applications. You can keep your employees' PCs, laptops, and smartphones current and you can contract with an Internet Service Provider (ISP) that provides the consistently highest and most reliable service, but, unlike with on-premise software, most of it is simply out of your hands.

New and Unproven

Salesforce.com signed up its first customers in 1999, more than a dozen years ago. Despite this, there's a perception that the cloud is too recent a development to be truly ready for prime time. Is this concern valid?

Perhaps partly. Certainly not completely. Yes, there are many new entrants to the world of cloud-based application providers. And it's inevitable that some of them will experience the glitches and growing pains of any new company. Yet a number of cloud providers have been around for a long time, either operating in the cloud or providing services or software for on-premise solutions. They've worked out most of their glitches before moving to the cloud, or have moved slowly to cloud solutions only after knowing they could offer a reliable service.

IS THE CLOUD A FAD?

Certainly, a lot of hype surrounds the cloud, but cut through that and you'll find compelling reasons behind the surge in its adoption (see *Chapter 3*). In addition, many cloud-based services have been up and running for over a decade and have proven themselves worthy. Take web-based email, for example, one of the first applications that businesses moved to the cloud. In 1997, Yahoo! launched Yahoo! Mail and Microsoft acquired Hotmail. Google's foray into email came a bit later with Gmail, premiering in 2004. But cloud-based offerings other than email have also been around for a while, such as online marketing provider Constant Contact, founded in 1998; payroll provider PayCycle, founded in 1999 (acquired by Intuit in 2009 and renamed Intuit Online Payroll); and web-conferencing provider WebEx, founded in 1997, to name only a few.

Still, every business needs to calculate what pain/benefit ratio it feels comfortable with. It could be that you'd save so much money, or improve employee efficiency to such a degree, that the risk of some unexpected downtime or software glitches is worth it. That's why so many new and small and medium businesses have embraced the cloud. Or you may have zero tolerance for any hiccups in a system your business depends on.

Financial Stability of Cloud Vendors

A related point to the "new and unproven" one above is that, by definition, cloud vendors *are* younger enterprises. And it's a fact that a lot of new businesses get acquired, change direction, or simply close up shop. If this happened after you had committed to using a particular SaaS or cloud service, at the very least you would be sorely inconvenienced, and at worst you'd lose critical data and experience a major business disruption.

Again, there's nothing unique about cloud companies that makes them more vulnerable to insolvency than makers of on-premise software. The newer cloud providers, however, like all new companies, are more apt to be acquired or go out of business than established on-premise solution providers. That's a function of their age, not of the fact that they're in the cloud.

The difference between cloud-based providers and on-premise providers is that *your* data is stored on *their* hardware. That makes you more vulnerable.

And it means you have to take some additional precautions to back up your data—either on your own premises, or to a different cloud-based solution.

You likely already have a process in place for vetting *any* potential vendors, to ensure that the products or services you are buying won't be "orphaned" due to bankruptcy. But, being participants in a relatively young industry, cloud vendors should probably be examined with special care. (See the worksheet on page 54 for hints on how to do this.)

WHAT IF I DON'T USE IT?

It's true that when you sign up for a cloud-based application, you'll incur an ongoing expense—an expense you'll pay whether you use the cloud service or not. But, as with any business purchase, you must first figure out what you need. So be sure, just as you would with on-premise software, to plan ahead (see *Chapter 7*). What functions do you need? What features would be nice but aren't necessarily mandatory? Who will use the software? What level of service do you require? Answer some key questions and you'll avoid headaches.

Internal Resistance

Moving to the cloud is not merely a technical shift. It's not even just a shift that affects business processes. It may also require a cultural transformation. After all, you're reducing the work load of your IT experts—whether internal or outsourced—and you're making your employees more accountable and their work more transparent. This can easily lead to getting pushback.

Larger enterprises with extensive in-house IT departments tend to have more trouble in this area than smaller ones. Their IT staffs can feel threatened when on-premise software, which they're responsible for managing, upgrading, and maintaining, is discontinued in favor of SaaS applications that require little or no staff support. They (not unreasonably) see their livelihoods threatened.

Although you may have only a few employees responsible for tech support, you could see similar pushback. Even if you can assure those employees that their jobs are safe, they can perceive a loss of organizational status. And, of course, it's your technologists' job to point out all the legitimate potential problems and vulnerabilities that have been mentioned in this chapter, so you can alert your workers to be vigilant in the cloud in order to keep the overall business safe. Be prepared for what can be a lively discussion.

Moreover, you may get pushback from employees who've relished the power they have by keeping all their valuable data or work product on their own computers, or even on paper. Imagine a successful salesperson who keeps all her contact info of customers and prospects in her own address

worksheet:

Validating the Financial Stability of a Cloud Vendor

Use this worksheet to investigate the financial stability of a cloud vendor you are considering. Go through the steps below and make notes on the information you find.

Vendor: _____

1. If the company is public, review its quarterly and annual financial statements, which can be easily found on its website, on Yahoo! Finance (http://finance.yahoo.com/), or on Google Finance (http://www.google.com/finance).

    _____

    _____

2. If the company is private, ask for whatever financial information it releases.

    _____

    _____

3. Request financial references, such as companies, organizations, or financial institutions with which the vendor has financial commitments.

    _____

    _____

4. Ask the vendor what percentage of its business comes from its best customer. _____

5. Do a detailed search of the company in major business publications and on websites such as the *Wall Street Journal, New York Times, Bloomberg*, or *BusinessWeek*. You may want to look at websites with local coverage, such as www.bizjournals.com, for companies that are too small to have received national coverage.

    _____

    _____

6. Check the company's ratings by major credit agencies, in particular Moody's and Standard & Poor's.

    _____

    _____

7. Research the firm's competitors—both in the cloud and in various on-premise markets.

    _____

    _____

book. She may feel threatened by having that data essentially taken and stored where others can retrieve it, especially in the event that she leaves.

In fact people often feel reluctant to change, no matter how beneficial that change might be. So expect some pushback and hesitation from your staff.

Switching Costs

Although one of the benefits of the cloud is that you can get your employees up and running much more quickly and easily than when installing on-premise software, the process of switching from an on-premise to a cloud solution can gobble up significant time and money.

You've got both technical and organizational issues to deal with. First, technical: In what format was the data in the on-premise software? Can it be easily uploaded to the cloud solution? Or will it require a good deal of manual intervention? What about connections to other systems (either other on-premise software or cloud applications) that your business uses? For example, does your on-premise inventory management system import data from your on-premise purchasing database? If so, you'll need to ensure that you can extract the same data and put it accurately into the new cloud-based inventory SaaS application.

Then, you have organizational considerations. You may find that the new cloud application forces you to rethink your business processes—and that your employees will have to adjust the way they perform their jobs. For example, when moving from an on-premise sales software package, like ACT!, to a SaaS CRM solution like salesforce.com, some businesses find that their sales and marketing employees collaborate much more closely than in the past. But they also can find that their sales professionals, used to keeping their own records on their own versions of ACT! on their own laptops, resent the transparency forced on them by a system in which their managers expect to see every customer phone call or email recorded.

Ironing out all the process changes and personnel issues can take much longer than the technical ones. Despite all this, managing organizational changes is not specific to the cloud, since any type of change can make employees nervous.

Integration with Other Business Data

Early users of cloud applications felt frustrated by their inability to easily integrate their other business data with the data stored in the cloud. In effect, these first cloud solutions created little islands of standalone data. You could analyze this data, run reports on it, set alerts that notified you when certain thresholds were reached. But you couldn't combine it with data in your other solutions, whether on-premise or cloud-based.

This is rapidly becoming a nonissue, particularly with the release of applications like Dell Boomi, a SaaS integration platform for cloud-to-cloud or cloud–to–on-premise application connectivity. (You'll learn more about integration in Chapter 9.)

Conclusion: Walk Before You Run

The number of small and medium–size businesses that have successfully migrated from on-premise to cloud applications is growing monthly. Indeed, many startups never even consider on-premise software, but jump straight to the cloud because of the financial and logistical advantages. If you're an existing company, though, you probably have made a fairly substantial investment in traditional software, and your business probably operates quite well on it. Yet sooner or later the time will come—perhaps when your current software requires a major and expensive upgrade—when the benefits of the cloud become so compelling that it's time to begin the transition. When that moment arrives, take careful steps. Consider all the potential issues raised in this chapter, and ask both yourself and your prospective cloud vendors all the recommended questions. You'll greatly increase the odds that your migration will be a successful one.

CLOUD FILE: INSIDER INSIGHT

Q *What's an unsung benefit of moving to the cloud?*

A Although cost reduction remains a key component of the cloud value proposition, agility is an equally if not more important reason to invest in cloud computing solutions. With our clients, we consistently find that the business benefits are oftentimes orders of magnitude more than the cost savings. It is the combination of business agility and cost savings the cloud-model provides that forms the foundation for innovation and business transformation. Companies that fail to recognize this will suboptimize their cloud investments—and risk being left behind by more nimble competitors.

Q *What should businesses do now to prepare for a move to the cloud?*

A **First, start small:** You don't need a full enterprise architecture to get started. Next time you find yourself setting up a spreadsheet to track some part of your business, sign up for a free Force.com account instead. You'll quickly get a taste for what's possible.

Second, think big: Once you're convinced of the potential, calculate how much you'd save, for example, by switching your email and file sharing to Google Apps. Start building a business-case-driven roadmap to the cloud.

Third, ask for help: Tap experts to move you to the cloud while you focus on the business at hand.

Q *What's your favorite customer success story?*

A Author Solutions is a midsize publishing company with $50 million in revenues and 400 employees. Working with Appirio, they moved their core business process—helping independent authors publish books—entirely to the cloud in just five months. (Read the full story in *InformationWeek*. http://www.informationweek.com/news/cloud-computing/software/210300262.)

continued

Company:
APPIRIO
www.appirio.com

Cloud Service:
ACCELERATING CLOUD ADOPTION

Insight provided by:
**RYAN NICHOLS,
SOLUTION MARKETING**

Appirio helps companies of all sizes build cloud-powered sales, service, and IT organizations. Appirio offers support throughout the cloud adoption lifecycle to help companies do more with cloud applications and platforms like salesforce.com, Google, and Workday.

CLOUD FILE: *continued*

Q *What causes cloud hesitation and how do you address it?*

A Some of the questions I hear are:

Is the cloud secure? Security concerns will always be top of mind, regardless of whether an application is on premise or in the cloud. Companies that have adopted cloud applications actually find that their cloud applications are at least as secure as their on-premise counterparts, if not more so. But cloud computing requires thinking about security in a different way: It's like moving your money from under your mattress to a bank. Your money is actually much more secure, even though it's not in your hands anymore (of course, you still need to pay careful attention to protect your PIN number and shred your bank statements!).

I'm on premise today—isn't it hard to move to the cloud? While a majority of corporate data may still be on-premise today, we would argue that most of the business processes and interactions that differentiate a company already lie outside their firewall. We live in a connected world where customers, prospects, partners, suppliers, developers, and employees are scattered across the globe, interacting with you on devices that you probably don't own, and on public forums and portals, that you might not control. Traditional on-premise applications were designed for the physical boundaries of yesterday's business models—cloud applications and platforms are optimized for today's networked, mobile workforce.

What if I get locked in? "Lock-in," whether to a vendor, a platform, a development environment, or a language, has been an issue for decades and used by numerous vendors as a reason why customers should or shouldn't move to a technology. We hear, "If it's not built using industry standards, you're locked in!" Maybe, but SQL is a standard, and you don't see a lot of companies regularly switching their databases. We hear, "If you don't control your data and apps in house, you're locked in!" Tell that to the companies paying millions to upgrade or rip out their legacy SAP and Lotus Notes.

Addressing Privacy and Security in the Cloud

By the end of this chapter...

you'll understand the sorts of privacy and security issues that arise when you use the cloud. You'll also know the right questions to ask to ensure that your digital assets are secure in the cloud.

Depositing Your Data

Using cloud services—which, by definition, means you're storing important business data and services on a cloud vendor's system and not on your own physical premises—is similar to depositing cash in a bank account.

You trust and depend on your bank to keep your money safe. Your money there is better protected from loss or theft than if you hid it under your mattress. You can still easily get your hands on your money when you need it—at the bank's physical branch office, through online funds transfer, by writing checks, or by going to an ATM—but the risk of loss or theft is significantly reduced. In the best of all worlds, all this is true about trusting your data to the cloud.

In both the case of the bank and the cloud, you've decided that a third party can protect your valuable assets better than you can on your own. And in both cases, you need to consider a variety of factors before choosing that third party—such as its reputation, the security safeguards it has put into place, and how easy it will be to access your assets once you've handed them over.

Cloud services and banks differ in one critical way. When you deposit your money in a bank, that bank (backed up by laws, regulations, and an entire financial services infrastructure developed over decades) assumes responsibility for protecting it.[1] But when you subscribe to cloud services, you must take at least partial responsibility for ensuring that your digital assets are safe. Actions you take, and decisions you make, directly affect the security, privacy, and availability of your data. That's why it's vital that you understand the precise risks and vulnerabilities that arise when you use the cloud—*and* how to work with your cloud vendor to best protect yourself.

Security and Privacy Risks in the Cloud

Early on, security—or, to be more precise, the perceived lack of it—deterred many businesses from committing to the cloud. Given how high the stakes are, this is understandable. No business can afford to have its customer list stolen, its financial records corrupted, or its highly sensitive personnel database exposed to the world. Today, many of these fears have been alleviated. Yet before moving a critical aspect of your business to the cloud, you should strictly perform your due diligence to make sure your cloud vendor is adequately protected.

You want to make certain your data is secure and that it will be there when you want it, whenever you want it. You also want to make sure it's private and kept away from any and all unauthorized eyes.

---

1. The FDIC—the Federal Deposit Insurance Corporation—is an independent agency of the U.S. government that protects depositors of insured banks located in the United States against the loss of their deposits if their bank fails.

TWO-FACTOR AUTHENTICATION: Any method of authenticating users of a system that requires users to present two pieces of evidence that proves they're indeed who they say they are. Evidence can include a password or personal identification number (PIN); a physical document such as a driver's license or passport; or biometric data, such as a fingerprint or retinal scan. Cloud applications don't require biometric or physical evidence to authenticate your users, for obvious reasons. In general, the strongest two-factor authentication methods include something a user knows (a password) along with something a user possesses (a passport or an ID). Usually, the second piece of evidence—after a password—is a security challenge question or an email verification link.

AUTHORIZATION: Ensures that authenticated individuals can access only the data you specify. Authorization affects many areas of SaaS applications, such as employees' abilities to view or edit files, add or delete users, or change the application in other ways.

The key security and privacy concerns you're likely to have include making sure that:

- Your data is not lost or corrupted.

- You are not locked out of your data.

- Your data is not accessed by anyone outside your organization unless you specifically authorize it.

- Employees only have access to data that is appropriate for their eyes.

- You can remove access when an employee leaves your company.

- The cloud provider has taken adequate security precautions internally.

- The cloud provider is stable and likely to be there in the future.

- Your data is backed up securely enough to survive any and all types of disasters—both natural and human-caused.

- You can take your data with you if you decide to change providers.

- Your data will be deleted if you sever your relationship with the cloud provider.

Therefore, when you start investigating cloud services, you need to make sure that the vendor can do the following:

- **Keep your data secure**

  Your data needs to be safe at all times. This means when it resides on your local device—whether that's a PC, a laptop, or a smartphone—as well as when it's stored in the cloud and when it's in transit between those places. It's critical to talk with your cloud vendor and find out what mechanisms are in place to protect your data.

  First, make sure your vendor encrypts data both when it's in transit and when it's at rest in the cloud. (Encryption is the process of transforming information so it can't be read or understood without a "key.")

  Second, If you're using a public, rather than private, cloud (see page 28), you need to ask your cloud vendor what methods it uses to ensure that your data is kept utterly secure, separate from the data of its other customers. (Remember, public clouds are "multitenant," in that they house data from a variety of businesses, similar to when you rent an apartment or office in a multistoried building that has other occupants. You don't want any other "tenants" of the cloud service getting access to your data.)

  Third, quiz the potential vendor about its own *internal* security practices. After all, one of the ironies of the cloud business model is that the biggest threats can come from within, rather than from outside, the cloud company. You're entrusting your cloud vendor with what in many cases are your data crown jewels. What safeguards has it put in place to prevent its own *employees* from plundering them? Take, for instance, payroll data. Cloud-based payroll services are increasingly popular among small and medium businesses that find the paperwork involved in processing payroll too onerous to do internally. But in sending payroll processing to the cloud, you're also sending your employees' names, social security numbers, addresses, phone numbers, and all sorts of other personal information, not to mention your business's bank account numbers and PINs.

WHAT MAKES A GOOD PASSWORD?

Usernames in combination with passwords are the most common security mechanisms to protect cloud services. Alas, it's relatively easy to figure out passwords—either through automated "password cracking" programs or by a savvy hacker who knows enough about an individual user's personal information to make a good guess. Here are some password best practices to share with your employees to prevent that from happening:

- **DON'T USE REAL WORDS, NAMES, OR PROPER NOUNS.** These are the types of passwords that are the most easily cracked by automated programs.

- **CREATE PASSWORDS OF AT LEAST SIX CHARACTERS OR NUMBERS IN LENGTH.** If the program allows, create even longer ones—more than eight characters or numbers is ideal.

- **USE AT LEAST TWO NUMBERS.** Positioning the numbers at the beginning of the password makes for a stronger password.

- **NEVER USE A STRING OF SEQUENTIAL NUMBERS OR LETTERS.** Passwords made up of 1-2-3-4 or a-b-c-d are unfortunately all too common, and easily broken.

- **NEVER USE A PERSONAL NUMBER ASSOCIATED WITH YOU.** This means no phone numbers, social security numbers, license plate numbers, and the like.

So, one of your questions to pose to any potential cloud vendor is: "What internal processes, procedures, and policies do you have about *your* employees' accessing my sensitive data?" There may be times—for example, if a customer support representative is helping you with a problem—that you want your vendor to be able to see what *you* see on your computer screen. But in such cases, clear rules should set the boundaries of who can open up your account, and what they can see. So one of your top priorities should be vetting the vendor's internal controls. After that, you will of course want to ask about security mechanisms for keeping external intruders out of the cloud data vaults.

NOTE: Bear in mind that keeping data safe means protecting against physical *as well as electronic break-ins. Hackers steal data by sneaking into systems over network connections. But if someone broke into a cloud vendor's data center and ran away with the physical server on which your data was stored, that would be equally devastating. So make sure that your cloud provider's data center is protected by such things*

"Be aware that many countries are putting laws and regulations in place that could impact your ability to use cloud applications. For example, Swiss companies cannot host their data outside the country. Germany is likely to follow suit. Moving to the cloud is more than a technical decision."

— Richard Giddey, vice president of StorageCraft's Asia-Pacific division

as high fences, 24/7 security patrols, video surveillance, ID badges, and other forms of identifying legitimate visitors or tenants (such as fingerprint checks or retinal scans).

- **Ensure that all users are properly authenticated**
  Authentication is about making sure that all the people who try to use the cloud service you've subscribed to are actually who they say they are. To authenticate users, your cloud vendor should demand "evidence" from anyone trying to access your data. This evidence can take the form of a username/password combination, a digital certificate, or even a "two-factor" authentication method (see page 61) that requires the user to provide both an answer to a security question in addition to a password, as in online banking. Your cloud vendor should also have security mechanisms in place to detect any efforts to fool the system. For example, too many failed attempts to enter a password should trigger the freezing of an account, or cause an alert to be sent to you.

- **Set proper levels of authorization**
  In addition to being authenticated, users must be *authorized*. Authorization is about ensuring that authenticated individuals can access *only* the data you want them to. For example, if you're using a cloud-based payroll service, you'd want most of your employees to only have the right to view their own financial records. But, as the owner of the company, you'd want the ability to see all records. And you will probably want to give broader access rights to your chief financial officer than to individual employees—though perhaps not as many rights as you have yourself. So an important question to ask your cloud vendor is how much flexibility you'll have to specify exactly what individual users can do.

Authorization affects many different levels of a SaaS application. For instance, you may allow some users to view data, but not edit it. You might allow some users to see other users' data and activities—say, managers or supervisors of a department. And you may allow certain users to make administrative changes or adjust the application itself, such as adding new users or a new type of customer account, or allow them to change other users' authorization status.

You also want to be able to change authorization at will—for example, if a member of your human resources (HR) staff, who previously had access to a broader-than-typical array of personnel records, moves over to the sales team, you'll want to be able to swiftly adjust that person's access rights accordingly. And, of course, if someone leaves the company, you need to be able to immediately cut off all access to the system for that person.

WHAT TO DO WHEN EMPLOYEES LEAVE

If you use a cloud service, employee turnover represents very real vulnerability. That's the point at which one of the strengths of using a cloud service—the fact that your employees can use it from remote locations, by a variety of devices—becomes a security risk. If you're terminating an employee, it's good practice to cut off access simultaneously with telling the employee of the termination. Even if you and an employee part ways amicably, it's essential to immediately cut off access to the cloud service for that employee by ending access to that account. If the employee who's leaving is disgruntled in any way, there's a special urgency to doing this. This action is just as important as collecting office keys and any equipment with which the employee has been entrusted.

NOTE: You aren't deleting the user account—you may need it to review if you have any questions about unfinished projects that employee may have been working on, or to examine activities. Instead, you're simply blocking access for the terminated employee. You should retain the right to access the account to maintain proper history and to audit records.

- **Monitor and track all user activity**
  Tracking all usage of the cloud service, and keeping a record of it, is critical. Your cloud vendor should give you the ability to audit all activity on your account at any point in time. You should be able to see which users accessed the cloud service, from what device, and when. You should be able to see which user was responsible for the last edit to a document. If you want more detailed information, that should be available as well, though you may need the vendor to pull specialized reports, since not all activity logs are available to you as the administrator.

worksheet:

Determining Employee Access Rights to Cloud Services

List each cloud service you're using or considering using across the top row, and name each employee (or type of employee) who will be using these services down the first column. Then fill in the grid based on which features of each cloud service each employee needs to access.

EMPLOYEE	CLOUD SERVICE	CLOUD SERVICE	CLOUD SERVICE

BRINGING THE CLOUD DOWN TO EARTH | *by Rhonda Abrams*

When you have this monitoring capability, if a question ever arises about who had access to certain information, or who changed a vital piece of data, you have a way to get answers.

- **Ensure compliance to laws, regulations, and guidelines as required by your particular business, industry, and geographical region**
  Compliance, according to dictionary.com, means "the act of conforming, acquiescing, or yielding," and in business, this has come to mean adhering to specific rules, laws, regulations, guidelines, and best practices. Compliance mandates vary from industry to industry, and region to region, but the general trend is that businesses are being required to follow an increasing number of legal requirements when collecting, processing, and storing information. For example, the Health Insurance Portability and Accountability Act (HIPAA) strictly limits what can be disclosed about individual consumers' health records by healthcare providers like physicians or hospitals or insurance companies. Any inadvertent violation of HIPAA requires the healthcare provider to immediately contact relevant authorities and affected individuals. Alternatively, the Right to Financial Privacy Act governs the release of customer financial information to federal authorities. Generally, the customer must receive notice before the information is released so the customer can challenge the release (this rule has some notable exceptions).

Typically, any company that routinely deals with personally identifiable information (PII)—that is, data that can uniquely identify individuals, such as full names coupled with addresses or phone numbers or social security numbers—must be extraordinarily careful to protect it from loss or theft. One of the most important requests you can make of a prospective cloud provider, therefore, is to supply details of its compliance program. Some of the standards and laws that you might want to ask about are the PCI standard[2] for the payment

---

2. "Payment Card Industry Data Security Standard," Wikipedia, http://en.wikipedia.org/wiki/Payment_Card_Industry_Data_Security_Standard.

card industry; HIPAA[3] for healthcare providers; SAS 70 (see sidebar below), which covers application security, physical security, and security processes; and ISO 27002,[4] which encompasses hundreds of options for security management.

- **Verify that when you delete data in the cloud, it's actually gone**
When you hit the Delete key on your computer, copies of the deleted material may still exist on your computer's hard drive or in externally stored backup copies of the data. This can also happen with your data in the cloud. When you decide to delete something, or when you want to terminate your use of a particular cloud vendor's service, you want *all* the data to be eliminated from existence.

- **Confirm that you own the data that resides in the cloud**
According to a 2011 report by the National Institute of Standards and Technology, issued by the U.S. Department of Commerce, titled "Guidelines on Security and Privacy in

WHAT IS SAS 70 AND WHY SHOULD I CARE?

The Statement on Auditing Standards No. 70 (SAS 70) was developed by the American Institute of Certified Public Accountants. It was designed to ensure that companies providing business services—as opposed to products—met rigorous quality standards.

The reason this matters to you? Cloud vendors, by definition, provide services rather than the products delivered by traditional on-premise software makers. You want to know that they've put sufficient safeguards and controls in place to protect and secure your data. If they've passed an SAS 70 audit, you can rest much easier.

Add "Have you passed an SAS 70 audit?" to your list of must-ask questions for any cloud vendors you are considering.

---

3. "Health Insurance Portability and Accountability Act," Wikipedia, http://en.wikipedia.org/wiki/Hipaa.

4. "The ISO 27000 Directory," 2008, http://www.27000.org/iso-27002.htm.

Public Cloud Computing,"[5] one of the most critical points you need to establish upfront with a cloud vendor is *ownership rights.* You should make sure you own your data: The cloud vendor has no rights whatsoever to access it, view it, or license it to others. Make sure this is spelled out in the contract with your cloud vendor, and do not permit your ownership rights to be diluted or tampered with in any way.

- **Establish service level agreements (SLAs) that specify data and system availability**
  For obvious reasons, you need to be able to access your data whenever you need it. This is where SLAs come in (see page 70). You may have to pay extra for SLAs that specify higher levels of availability. And typically, the vendor has to pay a penalty if it doesn't meet its SLA commitment in a given month.

- **Protect and secure your data in case of a disaster**
  Disasters do happen: hurricanes, tornadoes, floods, fires. But it doesn't take a disaster to make your data unavailable—even power outages can interrupt your ability to access your data. That's why your vendor should store your data in multiple locations. Ask your cloud provider what it does to protect your data and keep your service running in case of an adverse event—and, in worst-case scenarios, how it plans to recover and restore data and service in case of a disruption. Absolutely discuss where your data is stored—which countries or cities—and what redundant systems are in place. Avoid vendors that store all your data in a single system at a single location: You should not be satisfied unless the cloud vendor is replicating your data across multiple servers, networks, and regions. This is not negotiable.

factoid

Small and medium businesses' spending on cloud services will exceed $100 billion by 2014.[6]

---

5. "Guidelines on Security and Privacy in Public Cloud Computing," NIST, May, 2011, http://csrc.nist.gov/publications/nistir/ir7751/nistir-7751_2010-csd-annual-report.pdf.

6. "World Wide Cloud Services Study 2010," AMI Partners, August 19, 2010, http://www.crn.in/Software-019Aug010-SMB-Cloud-Spending-To-Approach-100-Billion-By-2014.aspx.

SERVICE LEVEL AGREEMENT (SLA) BEST PRACTICES

An SLA clarifies the responsibilities between the IT service provider and the customer, providing a framework and a common understanding for both parties. It is most effective when the IT service provider and the business customer collaborate on what should be included. This agreement becomes a guideline for managing the relationship between the customer and the IT service provider.

Because an SLA can be used to describe a variety of IT services, the particular elements included in the SLA will depend on the circumstances. A good SLA addresses the following:

- What service(s) are being made available to what customers?
- What level of service or quality of service should the customer expect?
- What are the costs to provide this level of service?
- How will the service be delivered?
- How will the service provider monitor or track and report on performance?
- When will the SLA be reviewed?

- **Enable a smooth exit**
  It happens to the best of vendor relationships: You decide to move on. Whether you're transitioning to a different cloud vendor, or have decided that you want to go back to an on-premise solution, you need to be able to easily and painlessly retrieve all your data and move it to a new location of your choice. Don't just assume this will be possible. Ask the cloud vendor what the process is for detaching from it. What's required? How long will it take? Will any extra fees or charges be assessed? And—most important—what format will the data be in when you retrieve it? Will you be able to easily flow it into a new system, or will it require tortuous data manipulation?

checklist:

Security Questions for Potential Cloud Service Providers

☐ What encryption mechanisms do you use for customers' data?

☐ In how many locations do you store customer data?

☐ What safeguards do you employ to ensure that different customers' data in a multitenant cloud is kept separate?

☐ How is your data center physically protected?

☐ Which of your employees have access to customers' data?

☐ How do you authenticate users?

☐ How precisely can you specify the degree of access that individual users have to data?

☐ What tracking, reporting, and auditing capabilities do you offer?

☐ Do you comply with all relevant government and industry laws and regulations?

☐ Have you passed an SAS 70 audit?

☐ What happens to data when you "delete" it? Is it actually wiped out?

☐ Who owns the rights to the data?

☐ What SLAs do you offer?

☐ How many and what types of security breaches have you experienced in the last 12 months? If you had any, what were they? What new protections have you put into place?

☐ What disaster recovery protections do you have in place?

☐ What are your security scenarios? Why should I trust you?

☐ What happens if we decide we want to discontinue using your services?

Perform Your Due Diligence in Cloud Security

Perfect security is not possible. Security always involves balancing the costs and hassle of implementing protective measures against the costs and hassle of a breach in which your data is lost or corrupted.

In the end, security is *your* responsibility. That's why you need to thoroughly review and understand the security policies and mechanisms of your potential cloud service providers. Unfortunately, when it comes to small businesses, many cloud vendors' service agreements are nonnegotiable. That makes it even more important to completely vet the terms and conditions and make sure they link up with your goals for your business processes.

An extremely useful resource for learning about and understanding the security risks and benefits of cloud computing is a report by the European Network and Information Security Agency titled "Cloud Computing: Benefits, Risks, and Recommendations for Information Security."[7] If you can tolerate a certain amount of jargon (keep a technical dictionary handy), the report does a good job of explaining 35 common security risks of cloud services, as well as strategies for mitigating them. The report makes useful recommendations for comparing cloud vendors' security policies and obtaining the necessary assurances that your data will indeed be secure.

It's worth repeating that perfect security is never achievable. Even the most prominent, pioneering security technology firms suffer occasional breaches.[8] That's why, no matter how solid your cloud vendor's security mechanisms seem to be, you need a contingency plan for when things go wrong.

9. *"Measuring Website Security: Windows of Exposure,"* White Hat Security, Winter 2011, https://www.whitehatsec.com/resource/whitepapers/cloud.html.

7. "Cloud Computing: Benefits, Risks, and Recommendations for Information Security," ENISA, November 20, 2009, http://www.enisa.europa.eu/act/rm/files/deliverables/cloud-computing-risk-assessment.

8. "Cyberattacks fuel concerns about RSA SecurID breach," Computerworld, June 1, 2011, http://www.computerworld.com/s/article/9217216/Cyberattacks_fuel_concerns_about_RSA_SecurID_breach.

CLOUD FILE: INSIDER INSIGHT

Q *What causes cloud hesitation and how do you address it?*

A While security and reliability are often cited as reasons for not moving to the cloud, most small and medium businesses really need a cloud solution that is easy to use. If you lack extensive technical teams, seek out ease of use as a priority.

Q *What's an unsung benefit of moving to the cloud?*

A While using SaaS applications is a great first step to "cloud enable" your company and reduce costs, using the "public cloud" to host your own application or development environment will greatly simplify management of your infrastructure. The least recognized benefit of moving to the cloud is how much easier it is to scale your infrastructure needs quickly.

Q *What should businesses do now to prepare for a move to the cloud?*

A Move at a pace that makes sense to you. To start, begin migrating noncustom applications (email, CRM, HR, benefits, project management, and the like) to the cloud. Then, experiment with moving your software testing environment to a cloud computing hosting company, such as OpSource or Amazon Web Services. Once you've gotten a feel for developing applications on servers in the cloud (not in your own data center), then move one of your production customer-facing or internal applications to the cloud.

Q *What will a typical small or medium IT infrastructure look like in 10 years?*

A Today's younger consumers use the cloud every day; they are on Facebook and Twitter and get the majority of their news and information online. They expect every application to run like the ones on their iPhone, iPad, or browser, delivering a constant stream of updates. In 10 years, these young consumers will be running companies of their own, and they will naturally expect easy-to-use, flexible IT infrastructure that lives in the cloud.

continued

Company:
OPSOURCE

www.opsource.net

Cloud Service:
**CLOUD HOSTING,
MANAGED HOSTING,
MANAGED SERVICES**

Insight provided by:
TREB RYAN, CEO

OpSource provides cloud and managed hosting solutions that enable businesses to accelerate growth and scale operations while controlling costs and IT infrastructure support risks. Companies rely on OpSource's technology to operate high-availability, business-critical hosting environments.

Q *What's your favorite customer success story?*

A A small online security services company was managing its own infrastructure within a leased data center. Every month, they were spending money on colocation space, power, bandwidth, and equipment leases. Due to lack of dedicated IT staff, one of their software developers was informally responsible for troubleshooting server problems. By moving all of their applications into the OpSource Cloud, they save $17,000 per month. In addition to improving their bottom line, application uptime improved and their customers were thrilled.

Financial Considerations and Return on Investment (ROI)

By the end of this chapter

you'll have found out how the benefits of the cloud translate into bottom-line results, and you'll have had an opportunity to calculate some actual numbers for your own business.

A New Way to Think about Technology Costs

You make financial decisions about ways to invest in and operate your business based on many factors. How a decision affects your profitability is paramount, but other considerations relate to that profitability: cash flow, cash reserves, fluctuations in market demand, and also tax law and accounting rules.

Deciding to switch from on-premise software (and, often, the accompanying additional hardware and databases required) to cloud-based solutions also enables small and medium businesses like yours to use a different financial model altogether. You go from capital expenses to operating expenses—represented by the monthly, quarterly, or annual fees you pay to cloud vendors for the right to use their SaaS applications and other cloud services. Thus, the need to pull together large amounts of cash for a purchase evaporates. Other advantages accrue: having predictable "fixed" costs rather than the variable costs that occur when you need to scramble to perform vendor-mandated upgrades or replace broken or outdated equipment; plus the ability to deduct from your taxes the full expense, rather than adhering to the IRS's limited-depreciation schedule.

These changes are far more than simply a matter of accounting procedures—they can have a direct, and ideally positive, impact on your bottom line. They can affect how much money you have available for building your business, how much you have in the bank at the end of the month, and how competitive you are in the marketplace.

Leasing and Licensing

Aren't some of these benefits the same as you'd get by leasing? Yes. And no. Leasing is primarily just a payment model, not a service model. You gain many of the cash and tax advantages of the cloud—no (or little) upfront large cash expenditure for a purchase, predictable cash flow, and the ability to treat leasing as an operating rather than capital expense. But the product you choose at the beginning of the lease is the same product you have available at the end. You aren't benefitting from new technology and upgrades. You're stuck with the same amount of product that you leased years ago, even if your needs have changed. You need to keep paying even if you decide the product isn't working for you anymore. And you may have to sign rigid service and maintenance agreements that impose constraints on your ability to customize the technology to meet your needs. Traditionally, leasing has been considered a good option for cash-strapped companies that are willing to pay more for stretching out payments over time. For example, a computer that would cost $4,000 to buy outright would cost $5,760 if leased for three years at $160 per month.[1]

Although some more recent total cost of ownership (TCO) studies have suggested that leasing computers is cheaper than

---

1. "Should You Lease or Buy Your Tech Equipment?" by Peter Alexander, Entrepreneur. com. http://www.entrepreneur.com/technology/techtrendscolumnistpeteralexander/ article80230.html.

CAPITAL EXPENDITURE: Traditionally, businesses have treated (and have been required by tax authorities to treat) technology acquisitions as capital expenditures: buying them outright and depreciating them over time. As a result, businesses can deduct only a portion of that expense from their taxes at the end of the year.

SOFTWARE LICENSE: A software license regulates the use of on-premise software, to prevent the pirating of software. Software is installed on individual machines and either licensed to specific users or controlled over the office network via a "license server."

LEASING: When on-premise software is leased, the purchaser pays monthly, rather than paying the entire software price tag upfront. Although many of the cash flow and tax benefits of leasing are the same for both on-premise and cloud solutions, leasing is merely a payment model. The on-premise software product is the same, whether leased or purchased outright.

purchasing them outright once all the servicing, support, and related usage costs are included,[2] in fact the majority of small and medium businesses still prefer to purchase their hardware and software outright.

By moving to the cloud, businesses get the financial benefits of leasing—the predictable monthly costs, the ability to deduct those costs as operating expenses, and the opportunity to conserve cash—without the drawbacks. Of course, the relative costs and benefits and return on investment (ROI) will vary, based on the specific cloud solution under consideration. But on average, the cost of a cloud solution when compared to an on-premise or leased alternative will be significantly lower.

Another way that your cost model changes is related to how you pay for software. SaaS applications typically involve a recurring fee (monthly, quarterly, or yearly). Yet on-premise software is sold under software licensing agreements, the management of which can both be time-consuming and represent a hidden cost. For example, some software, like Microsoft Office, is installed on individual machines (desktop or laptop PCs), and is licensed to be used by a specific person on

---

2. "PC Total Cost of Ownership (TCO) and Leasing: The Realities of Reducing PC Ownership Costs," by Adam Braunstein, Robert Frances Group, May 10, 2007. http://www.rfgonline.com/events/rfg_pctco_051007_0.pdf.

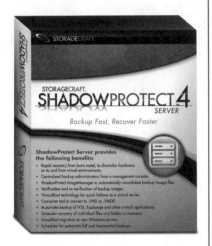

"It's amazing how quickly people can pick up cloud applications," Giddey said. "They're used to the browser interface, they know how to use it, and it's so much easier than trying to learn a new on-premise application."

StorageCraft Technology Corporation
Richard Giddey, Vice President Asia Pacific

BACKGROUND

Founded in 2003, StorageCraft Technology Corporation provides disk-based backup, disaster recovery, data protection, migration, and security solutions to businesses of all sizes. Although headquartered in Draper, Utah, the company has rapidly achieved a global presence due to its reputation for high-quality products, service, and technical innovation.

CHALLENGE

Richard Giddey, vice president of StorageCraft's Asia-Pacific division, oversees 30 workers from regional headquarters in Brisbane, Australia. As one of StorageCraft's first employees in 2003, Giddey was charged with establishing the firm's presence and brand in a highly competitive marketplace for storage and backup solutions. One of his first challenges was to decide what technology he needed to support his mission.

"When we kicked off, our basic need was for a database for our business information," he said. He evaluated solutions from Oracle, Microsoft, and other database vendors, but they didn't meet his main criteria. "We knew we'd have a number of scattered branch offices throughout the region, and we needed to link all our data together while providing access to that data from anywhere," he continued. "It had to be quick and easy to use, otherwise—as we'd learned from experience—no one would bother to update it. Plus, given that most of us are on the road three weeks per month, it had to work just as fast from a remote location, using a laptop, as in the office."

Although the need to collect sales and customer data was his top priority at the beginning, "We knew we would eventually need an application that would help us with other business activities, such as marketing and customer support," said Giddey. "So we needed a solution that was very flexible, and which could be expanded and used in a variety of ways."

SOLUTION

The answer was the cloud. Today, the compay has a portfolio of applications that are nearly 100 percent cloud, with more than a dozen SaaS applications and cloud services ranging from salesforce.com and Vertical Response to Constant Contact, Webcom, LogMeIn, and Skype. "And this doesn't count all the social media we use every day," said Giddey.

Giddey started out slowly by using Salesforce CRM to collect contact information of sales prospects and potential distribution partners. "Anyone we met at any trade show, we put their name, address and phone number into salesforce.com," said Giddey. And the list continued to grow. His team started logging all customer support calls, along with solutions and fixes. From there it was easy to begin leveraging the data to execute email marketing campaigns.

It wasn't long, though, before Giddey realized that having so many standalone "islands" of information—even if individually they were easily accessible via the cloud—was not enough. He needed a way to tie them together. "We especially wanted to connect salesforce.com to QuickBooks, one of the few on-premise applications we use," he said. He consulted a third-party integrator, an expert on both Salesforce and Dell Boomi, who customized an integration to fit Giddey's precise needs.

Giddey felt a bit of sticker shock when told how much it would cost to do the integration, he admitted. "But then we thought about it. I'd been through integration exercises before. I thoroughly understood all the potential pitfalls," he said. "In particular, I knew how important testing was—and how time-consuming. Given that we would be depending on the integration for important accounting and billing functions, I knew we couldn't take a chance. I was right. They did a fantastic job. And the benefits we received made it a wise investment."

Still, Giddey feels that some applications aren't ready for the cloud. Standard office applications, such as word processing, spreadsheets, and presentation software, for example, are still best delivered on premise, Giddey believes. "And scalability is important—not all cloud applications can meet our projections for growth. And, given the fact that our Internet bandwidth in Australia isn't the best, we've run into some performance issues."

Even so, Giddey is a big believer that the cloud is the future—so much so that StorageCraft will step into the market and offer its own customers cloud-based solutions. "It's only a matter of time," he said.

BENEFITS

Today, more than 80,000 contacts are stored in StorageCraft's Asia-Pacific Salesforce CRM application. All the support data captured over the years has proven invaluable, as StorageCraft now publishes advice derived from this data on its website.

Because of the rapid pace of the growth of StorageCraft, the fact that Giddey can get new employees up and running quickly using salesforce.com's online training module is critical. "It's amazing how quickly people can pick up cloud applications," he said. "They're used to the browser interface, they know how to use it, and it's so much easier than trying to learn a new on-premise application."

And with Constant Contact and Vertical Response as part of the mix, Giddey can put together sophisticated marketing campaigns and immediately get feedback on how successful they are at generating actual sales. The fact that all these applications are integrated to each other, with connections to QuickBooks financial data as well, means that Giddey can run a tight, cost-effective operation. ■

a specific device. Use of other on-premise applications, like computer-aided design (CAD) software, although installed on many individual machines, is controlled over the office network via something called a "license server." If you've installed 10 copies of Pro/Engineer CAD software in your offices, but only purchased five licenses, a maximum of five of your engineers can use the software at a given time. Other software, like enterprise resource planning (ERP) systems, is also licensed to a particular number of users, but it's your job to monitor that the license isn't being violated. If the vendor ever audits your offices and finds violations, you could face steep fines. In addition, many multiuser on-premise applications include databases to store data. All this adds up to your needing more—and more expert—IT help to manage business applications. You need a desktop administrator, a systems administrator, a database administrator, and a network administrator. All these personnel costs figure into any ROI calculation.

Passing the Savings On

Moreover—and this is vital—cloud-based offerings represent a different business model for your vendor, not just for you. This new business model enables vendors to provide software to you at a lower monthly cost. With the traditional business model, a software vendor had to make an initial sale, work on upgrades for years, and then market and push upgrade sales. A graph of its income pattern would look like a snake eating a mouse: a big bulge followed by flat lines. By

UP-TO-DATE AND UNINTERRUPTED

Moving to the cloud means you'll have tools and continually updated software available for you and your staff without the expense and disruption—the spikes and learning curve—of a major upgrade. Many companies, both large and small, work on tools that may be five or more years out of date because they can't afford, either financially or operationally, to upgrade. Ask yourself: How much does it cost *you* to be less competitive and less efficient?

providing software as a service, it gets predictable cash flow and is able to make continual, incremental improvements to keep up with technological changes. Because its product is Internet rather than operating system-based, it's spared the considerable expense of developing different versions to work on different operating systems (or different versions of the same operating system). It can offer customers more while charging less.

Crunching the Numbers

To begin comparing the cost of a cloud versus an on-premise solution, it's beneficial to examine the main categories of expenses you'll encounter when choosing and using software.

- **Application purchase price**
  This is the upfront expense of acquiring the product initially, either for your entire company or for new employees. This can be substantial. This expense obviously applies only to on-premise software, because with SaaS applications and cloud services you're not buying an actual product.

- **Software upgrades**
  Once you have acquired software, you'll also face the expense of the upgrades. Software manufacturers typically release upgrades in cycles. For example, Microsoft updates its Office suite every three years; CAD systems typically are updated annually. One of the main benefits of cloud-based applications is that they shield you from the many expenses and complications of the on-premise software upgrade. Such upgrades are costly. Although some on-premise vendors charge an annual "maintenance fee" that includes all bug fixes and upgrades, others require you to purchase the new version of the application, install it on every user's machine, and then retrain each user—typically resulting in significant lost worker productivity until users master the new functionality.

  With cloud-based applications, you avoid most of that. Although cloud vendors (of course) constantly enhance their applications' functionality and usability, and users (of course)

factoid

In 1959, Bank of America installed the Electronic Recording Machine, Accounting (ERMA) to automate account processing. The machine-readable, magnetic ink font developed for ERMA is still used to this day in the world banking system. ERMA's ability to work 24/7, process 33,000 accounts per hour, and share data "online" across branches, revolutionized the banking industry.

need to be trained when such changes are implemented, the whole experience is dramatically less disruptive.

- **Operating system upgrades**
Your on-premise software must work—and work well—with the current version of your on-premise operating system. It's not uncommon for an application vendor to release a new version that not only forces customers to pay an upgrade fee (see above), but then also requires a costly operating system upgrade to be compatible. The reverse is also true: You acquire a new operating system, and then you must upgrade your software to be compatible. Unfortunately, these may not occur simultaneously. For instance, your operating system may be upgraded before a new version of your on-premise software is available, meaning significant disruption. The good news: Cloud-based solutions eliminate virtually all these operating system upgrade conflicts and costs.

- **Configuration/implementation services**
These expenses include one-time fees for services to help you set up and configure a system (custom fields and workflows), and to move data from the old system to the new one. Costs are similar for on-premise and cloud-based systems.

- **Hardware requirements**
Your employees will need some type of hardware device to actually use the application. In many cases, the hardware cost of deploying an on-premise and a cloud solution will be roughly equivalent, especially for individual users. In some cases, though, a particular on-premise application will require additional or special hardware: more servers, a more powerful processor, or more memory, for example. Conversely, moving to cloud-based solutions may mean that you no longer need as much central storage or server hardware. Such savings (or costs) should be taken into account.

- **Software maintenance, IT, and support**

  What does it cost you to maintain and service your on-premise software? On-premise software is rarely trouble-free. You may pay for maintenance through a required annual maintenance fee; employ your own internal IT support experts; hire outside contractors; or contract with your application vendor for premium technical support service. Whatever route you take, these costs add up. You may also purchase additional tech support from a cloud provider, but cloud-based solutions are likely to trim your overall IT expenses, perhaps substantially.

- **Contract management services**

  Although every vendor relationship has to be managed in some way, cloud vendors—especially when mission-critical applications are involved—require a higher level of monitoring the level of usage. You want to ensure that you aren't paying for higher capacity than you need, to confirm that the SLAs are being met, and in general monitor the relationship. How much more time this will take, and how senior a person this mandates, depends on the nature of the cloud-based solutions you choose. Keep in mind that although you don't need to monitor your on-premise vendor relationships quite so closely, you have to do a lot of tasks yourself that a cloud vendor would take care of for you. For example, you need to make certain that your on-premise solution is constantly available to users. And you need to put measures in place to prevent outages and downtime.

- **Security systems and procedures**

  Using a cloud-based solution does *not* mean you can stop worrying about security—whether it's your own or the quality of the vendor's. Because you're doing more of your business over the Internet, you'll probably spend more time—and thus more money—guaranteeing that you have adequate security systems and procedures in place. You'll also spend a bit more time ensuring that your SaaS vendor is maintaining its security levels. According to a 2010 PricewaterhouseCoopers survey, significantly fewer

factoid

Cloud computing is being adopted by businesses at a pace far exceeding projections. According to research by Morgan Stanley's Alphawise service, the proportion of global enterprises using the cloud will rise from 28 percent to 51 percent between 2011 and 2014, which will represent a more than doubling of the actual workloads running in the cloud (from 10 percent to 22 percent). [3]

3. "Cloud Computing Takes Off: Market Set to Boom as Migration Accelerates," Morgan Stanley Research Global, May 23, 2011, http://www.morganstanley.com/views/perspectives/cloud_computing.pdf.

companies than in previous years were very confident that their business partners and suppliers had security that met their own internal standards.[4] The implications of this: Companies will need to spend more time and money verifying the security mechanisms and quality of cloud vendors than they would with on-premise software.[5] One thing that balances this out, however, is that you typically eliminate your own data backup solution, since most SaaS vendors automatically include remote backup of data as part of their services.

- **Miscellaneous transition/migration**
  Unless you are a startup that has just opened its doors, you'll have to swallow data migration costs. This is the case whether you're moving from one on-premise solution to another; migrating from an on-premise solution to a SaaS one; or even using a manual process that depends on individual employees' contributing data they "own"—for example, standalone Excel spreadsheets maintained on their desktops. Even routine software upgrades can create data migration challenges if the vendor has significantly changed the way it stores data. Included in all this is the benefit that you rarely just swap out one application for another—usually you're tweaking or improving your underlying business processes so you can get the most out of the new solution. And all migration projects require you to carefully "clean" your existing data before putting it in the new system. (For more on migration, see Chapter 8.)

- **Training users**
  As previously noted (see page 34), SaaS applications are designed and tend to be more user-friendly and intuitive than on-premise software, thus requiring less training. What

---

4. "Global State of Information Security Survey," PricewaterhouseCoopers, 2010. http:/www.pwc.com/gx/en/information-security-survey.

5. "Calculating Cloud ROI Is Harder Than It Looks," by Mary Shacklett, Dell.com, October 19, 2010. http://content.dell.com/us/en/enterprise/d/large-business/calculating-cloud-roi.aspx.

training *is* necessary can usually be completed online at the users' convenience rather than requiring travel or missed work days. Additionally, if individual users have questions, they can usually contact the cloud vendor's support staff directly without involving an internal IT person or consultant, saving even more money.

A BUSINESS-CENTRIC LOOK AT CLOUD ROI

In 2010, the Open Group published a landmark white paper, "Building Return on Investment from Cloud Computing," which argued that to get a realistic handle on cloud ROI, companies must measure how it improved key business-centric metrics. The paper's lead author, Mark Skilton, the director of research firm Capgemini, identified eight of these metrics in an article for *CIO Magazine*.[6] In essence, according to Skilton, businesses should try to quantify the financial impact of the following business advantages:

1. Keeping up with the rate of technological and business change
2. Minimizing the total cost of ownership of a technology solution
3. Getting users up and running quickly and easily
4. Maintaining better control over costs and profit margins
5. Scaling use of a technology up and down as the business requires
6. Improving the ability to comply with "green" goals and mandates
7. Avoiding over- or under-buying of technology when compared to actual business needs
8. Improving business skills, knowledge, and capabilities

The Hidden Costs of Falling behind the Technology Curve

One of the most difficult things to put a number to in business is "opportunity cost." Think back: What was the cost to *your* business of missing an opportunity?

You can miss opportunities for many reasons. Your employees lack the skills required to bid on a particular job. Or, you have skilled employees, but not enough of them. Or, your operating costs are so high that you priced yourself out of the market. Or, you aren't able to deliver the quality of product or service required by customers. Or, employees leave your

6. "Eight Ways to Measure Cloud ROI," by Mark Skilton, CIO, May 26, 2010. http://www.cio.com/article/595179/8_Ways_to_Measure_Cloud_ROI.

worksheet:

Comparing the Cost of a Cloud Solution to an On-Premise Solution

Fill out the worksheet below to examine the costs of cloud and on-premise applications.

COSTS	CLOUD APPLICATION 1	ON-PREMISE APPLICATION 1	CLOUD APPLICATION 2	ON-PREMISE APPLICATION 2
Application purchase price				
Software upgrades				
Operating system upgrades				
Configuration/ implementation services				
Hardware requirements				
Software maintenance, IT, and support				
Contract management services				
Security systems and procedures				
Miscellaneous transition/ migration				
Training users				
Other:				

business—voluntarily or involuntarily—and their knowledge walks out the door with them. In such cases, if they've been using a desktop-based application such as a complex Excel spreadsheet that they've programmed to include data merged from a number of sources and sophisticated calculations, you lose valuable data as well.

Lacking adequate technology support for your employees and business processes could contribute to any of these lost opportunities. And the list could go on. Your workers lose time and productivity because they have to enter data manually into multiple systems, or because they lack access to systems and data when on the road. By manually performing tasks that your competitors have successfully automated, or by lacking the capacity to ramp up to meet growing demand, or by having too-high overhead to competitively price your products or services, you set yourself up for significant opportunity cost losses.

COST-EFFECTIVE TIMING FOR CLOUD TRANSITIONS

Like many organizations, San Francisco-based nonprofit TechSoup has significant investments in a number of legacy applications that continue to work well. Eventually however, the time for a major upgrade will come, along with significant disruption. Pleased with its past successful adoptions of several cloud solutions, today, whether TechSoup needs an upgrade to its existing on-premise software or a brand-new type of application, the cloud is the first thought.

Co-CEO Marnie Webb expects infrastructure limitations to drive TechSoup to adopt cloud solutions more and more. "Eventually, the volume of data and transactions in our on-premise systems will tip us over," she said. "We'll be looking to host the data in the cloud, to crunch it more efficiently and effectively offsite."

Cloud-based solutions address many of these issues. So even after you calculate the expense of on-premise versus cloud, keep in mind that you can seize numerous, less-easily-quantifiable opportunities to increase revenues when you use this new way of deploying technology.

Company:
MARKETO

www.marketo.com

Cloud Service:
MARKETING AND SALES

Insight provided by:
JON MILLER, VP MARKETING
AND COFOUNDER

Marketo helps companies embrace the new transparent relationship between buyers and sellers, to drive revenue with greater efficiency than ever before. Marketo helps generate more leads, prioritize marketing spend, and aim sales resources to close the right deals faster.

Q *What's an unsung benefit of moving to the cloud?*

A The complete sharing of information across groups, divisions and geographies. There are often silos in businesses, but the cloud makes it seamless to share information across silos, and the cost of tying silos together is borne by the SaaS providers. For example, marketing applications can integrate with CRM solutions to share data that enables your sales team to update the marketing team while marketing helps sales learn about current and recent events. In a big company, this information is held in two very different databases that don't tie together. In the cloud, these two services tie together very well.

Q *What causes cloud hesitation and how do you address it?*

A Marketing professionals worry about loss of control, privacy issues, losing credit card information, and losing customer lists to competitors. In reality, the risk really isn't that high. It's as safe as using the web to check your bank balance or buy something on Amazon. We have the highest levels of security built in to our offerings from the ground up.

Q *What should businesses do now to prepare for a move to the cloud?*

A Just do it! As companies look to increase their performance while keeping costs and infrastructure in line, cloud-based solutions are the most logical choice.

Q *What will a typical small or medium IT infrastructure look like in 10 years?*

A Cloud companies didn't exist 10 years ago, and today they serve millions of businesses and have changed the game. Even the big players in the IT space are moving into the cloud. It's not too big a stretch to say that the vast majority of new investment will be in the cloud.

Strategic Planning: Your Customized Journey to the Cloud

By the end of this chapter...

you'll know how to evaluate your business needs and put together a cloud strategy that will benefit your business.

Your Road Map to the Cloud

By now you have a good idea of the business advantages of cloud-based applications (Chapter 3), as well as a sense of their potential risks (Chapter 4). You've done an initial financial assessment of how cloud solutions compare to the traditional on-premise ones (or the manual business processes) that you currently use (page 86). And you've decided to take the next steps toward actually implementing cloud solutions.

Now it's time to assess which aspects of your business can benefit most from the cloud, after which you need to begin evaluating specific cloud solutions that match your business needs. Then you'll be able to create a strategic road map for cloud implementation.

Keep in mind that, unless yours is a new business, transitioning to cloud-based services is a journey. It's not likely, or necessarily advisable, for you to move all your applications to the cloud in one fell swoop. As you examine your needs and the cloud-based offerings, you'll want to look at which business functions you want to move to the cloud earlier and which you'll move later.

BRINGING THE CLOUD DOWN TO EARTH

Throughout the planning process—especially as you begin researching actual cloud applications and services—don't allow yourself to get distracted by too much tech talk. Whatever cloud solutions you end up implementing should be chosen based on business criteria, not on hype, and certainly not on the fact that the cloud is the Next Big Thing.

Imagine that a new retail superstore has opened in your area that offers the widest and most contemporary selection of office furniture, equipment, briefcases and other accessories, even business clothes for both men and women, at prices that are lower than other stores. Would you automatically replace all your existing possessions you use to conduct your daily business? Of course not.

You'd take into account that you already have a large investment in the sorts of things the new store sells, and that many, if not most, of those things are still perfectly adequate for your requirements. So you'd assess your needs to see what—if anything—you lack, or what products already in your office or wardrobe need to be replaced, and then you'd begin putting together a list and doing some comparison shopping of the items to purchase first. At the same time, you'd certainly start thinking ahead to future scenarios in which you will need to upgrade or replace existing assets—and will take your time to shop around and verify that the new store indeed offers price or quality or other advantages over your previous suppliers. This is how you should approach the cloud.

Step One: Assess Your Actual Business Needs

Cloud solutions are not a panacea for every business problem you have. Yet they can address an impressively wide range of challenges that small and medium businesses face every day. Here are some of the issues you may be struggling with for which the cloud could provide relief.

- **Cut costs**
  Since this is a nearly universal goal for smaller businesses (indeed, businesses of any size), chances are good that you're always searching for ways to achieve this. As discussed on pages 30-32, the cloud model delivers cost savings in a number of ways, including a lower overall price tag when compared to on-premise solutions, and tax relief. Again, it might not make sense to rip out an on-premise application that's currently functional. But when you approach a natural decision point—such as when your software vendor forces you to undergo a pricey upgrade—that would be a great time to

consider an alternative cloud solution. If, by contrast, you realize that your operational costs are high due to the fact that manual processes make your employees very inefficient at doing their jobs—say, they're manually entering data into multiple software programs and printing out paper copies of reports to circulate to management—then automating and streamlining business processes using a cloud solution could result in significant cost savings.

- **Improve cash flow**
While related, this is a different issue than the previous one (cutting costs). You could be operating profitably from a cost perspective, yet are finding it difficult to amass cash in the bank to make necessary business expenditures. If your business is tight on cash, and (again) if you're under the gun to upgrade a mission-critical software application, that's a prime time to consider the cloud. You won't need to raise the thousands (or more) of dollars to purchase the software outright. In most cases, you won't incur the other expenses associated with a major software upgrade, such as hardware and operating systems upgrades and use of consultants to make sure the solution is customized to fit your needs. The huge upfront cash outlay gets transformed into a much more manageable fee that you pay at regular intervals: per month, per quarter, or sometimes per year. And since cloud-based solutions are paid on a predictable schedule, you even out cash flow, giving you much more clarity when trying to do projections and budgets.

learn the lingo

CONTENT MANAGEMENT: The management, backup, storage, and protection of data—documents, video, images, and other files—that ensures users always have the most up-to-date versions.

VOICE OVER INTERNET PROTOCOL (VoIP): Sends voice signals over the Internet using the same network your data flows over. VoIP makes it possible to place phone calls, send faxes, record conversations, hold multiparty conference calls, and more, over the Internet.

1. "TV Broadcast Satellite," *Popular Science*, May 1970, http://www.popsci.com/archive-viewer?id=8QAAAAAMBAJ&pg=66&query=a+c+clarke.

- **Enhance customer relationships**

  Keeping customers satisfied is critical to the success of any business. If you're like most businesses, you know there's always room for improving those all-important relationships. Perhaps your employees are still scrambling to pull paper files out of physical filing cabinets to look up customers' sales histories when they get a service call. Or your invoices, which are created by manually retrieving data from multiple systems, consistently contain errors that your customers have to bug you to fix. Or you realize your sales and marketing teams aren't following up on promotions, or are letting customer contracts expire without proactively seeking renewals. Cloud solutions are available to help with each and every one of these customer-related challenges—including a broad array of customer relationship management (CRM) solutions, such as Salesforce CRM, and integration tools, such as the Dell Boomi integration platform, that can tie together disparate solutions so critical customer info can be consolidated and nothing falls through the cracks.

- **Make better business decisions**

  Having access to timely, accurate, information is key to good decision-making. As you automate more and more aspects of your business, the amount of information available to you keeps increasing. Yet most small businesses struggle to make sense of all this information. It can be too much of a good thing, especially if your different software applications can't "talk" to one another. You can miss important trends or patterns. For example, you might be able to tell from your sales software that a certain product you make is flying off the shelves. But if you don't also consult your materials database, you won't see that your inventory of a certain ingredient needed to make that product is dangerously low. And you wouldn't know that your supplier doesn't expect to be able to deliver a new batch of that ingredient for six months unless you ask your purchasing manager to look into the standalone Excel spreadsheet on the departmental PC. Without the ability to connect the dots—between different software applications as well as between manual and automated processes—you could find yourself in trouble, despite virtually drowning in data. By moving to the cloud, you can create a central repository of information that integrates data from a broad range of systems and puts it at the fingertips of every employee who needs it.

- **Boost employee productivity**
  If your employees are spending too much time doing repetitive or manual data entry or consolidating information from various systems, or if anything that takes them away from their desktop PC—whether being home caring for a sick child, or on the road for a business conference—curtails their ability to do their jobs, then definitely consider the cloud. As mentioned in the previous point, the fact that cloud applications can be integrated tightly (with each other and with on-premise software), coupled with your employees' ability to ubiquitously access them from anywhere in the world where they have an Internet connection, makes employees infinitely more productive than if they were tied to on-premise software or manual processes.

- **Encourage collaboration**
  Helping employees share information with each other and work closely together—not to mention better serving customers, suppliers, and other business partners—is an increasingly common goal of smaller enterprises. This can be difficult with traditional on-premise software, and exceedingly inefficient if you're still working with paper documents. If your workforce is scattered geographically, the challenge is even harder to solve. Luckily, the cloud makes it easy for teams or workgroups to collaborate on tasks. Unlike many traditional software applications, you can have multiple users accessing the same data simultaneously, and even making changes in real time, no matter where they happen to be situated. You can enable collaboration with customers and business partners as well. For example, if you run a consulting business that requires continuous interaction with customers,

you can use the cloud to create common online "workspaces," rather than laboriously emailing documents back and forth.

- **Improve management and protection of critical company data**
  Some of the more popular cloud applications on the market are specifically targeted to help businesses better manage their data, as well as back it up and store it offsite to protect it from loss or corruption. These applications allow you to design workflow and other processes for moving data or content between various employees or other software solutions that ensure that users always have the most up-to-date version of critical data. Other solutions are available that automatically copy business data and store it away from your physical premises. That way, in case of disaster or theft in your office, you always have a "clean," safe copy of your data to retrieve. Cloud-based services also help make sure you get key information off individual employees' desks or computers and into secure company storage space. For example, individual employees may have customer information, projects, or presentations only on their own computers, making it hard or impossible for you to access, especially if they leave.

IN HOUSE OR IN THE CLOUD?

When determining whether to leave your data onsite or move it to the cloud, answer a few questions: First, do you need to access data remotely when away from the office? If not, consider leaving it in house. Or do you need to retrieve it while on the go? Then consider moving it to the cloud. Finally, how many users will you have, and are they located in the same place? If all the employees who'll be using the SaaS application are in your headquarters building and usually work at their desks, then moving to the cloud wouldn't be as obviously the right choice as if you had multiple users scattered all around the country or globe.

worksheet:

Identify Your Business Challenges

Use this worksheet to identify your particular business challenges, track how you are addressing them, and determine their urgency.

BUSINESS CHALLENGE	IN WHAT SPECIFIC WAYS DOES THIS PROBLEM PLAY OUT IN YOUR BUSINESS?	HAVE YOU IMPLEMENTED ANY TECH-NOLOGIES TO ADDRESS THIS PROBLEM?	IF YES, IN WHAT WAYS DOES YOUR CURRENT SOLUTION FAIL TO ADDRESS THE PROBLEM? IF NO, DESCRIBE THE MANUAL PROCESSES THAT ARE CONTRIBUT-ING TO THE PROBLEM.	HOW URGENT IS THE PROBLEM? *
Cut costs		☐ Yes ☐ No		☐ Very ☐ Somewhat ☐ Not Urgent
Improve cash flow		☐ Yes ☐ No		☐ Very ☐ Somewhat ☐ Not Urgent
Enhance customer relationships		☐ Yes ☐ No		☐ Very ☐ Somewhat ☐ Not Urgent
Make better business decisions		☐ Yes ☐ No		☐ Very ☐ Somewhat ☐ Not Urgent
Boost employee productivity		☐ Yes ☐ No		☐ Very ☐ Somewhat ☐ Not Urgent
Encourage collaboration		☐ Yes ☐ No		☐ Very ☐ Somewhat ☐ Not Urgent
Manage and protect critical data		☐ Yes ☐ No		☐ Very ☐ Somewhat ☐ Not Urgent
Other:		☐ Yes ☐ No		☐ Very ☐ Somewhat ☐ Not Urgent

* VERY (needs to be addressed ASAP); SOMEWHAT (needs solution within six months); NOT URGENT (can take my time finding the right solution)

Step Two: Research Which Cloud Services Are Available

Now that you've identified some areas of your business that might benefit from cloud solutions, it's time to begin looking at the solutions themselves. Here's a roundup of the type of cloud applications and services currently available. Since new ones appear on the market every month, this is far from a comprehensive list. But it does give you an idea of the type of solutions that are out there. For an up-to-date list, go to CrunchBase (http://www.crunchbase.com/tag/saas), which is a cloud-based (of course!) database of currently available cloud applications.

- **Financial**
  Whether you're looking for a better way to automate your billing, invoicing, payment processing, payroll, bookkeeping, or financial planning, solutions exist that enable you to do this in the cloud. Anything related to accounting or financial transactions falls into this category. Vendors that provide cloud-based financial applications include Intuit; Zephyr Financial Technologies; and Rebirth Financial.

- **Business Intelligence (BI)**
  Because cloud-based integration tools such as Dell Boomi make it possible to extract data from a broad range of on-premise and online (cloud) applications, business intelligence is a particularly rich category of cloud solutions. These tools help businesses analyze data and create reports that both illuminate business opportunities and analyze challenges. Typically, business intelligence applications take data that has been created and stored in other applications, import it, and provide user-friendly ways to slice and dice it. Vendors that provide cloud-based BI tools include Good-Data; Oco Inc.; and Actuate.

- **Collaboration**
  These tools allow users to share knowledge with others—whether between one individual and another, within workgroups, or even among separate businesses. Cloud vendors

that offer these applications include HyperOffice; CSC; and GroupSwim.

- **Customer Relationship Management (CRM)**
  These online services integrate information about customers, covering every aspect of sales, marketing, and customer service operations. Vendors providing these types of SaaS applications and cloud services include salesforce.com; Oracle; and Zoho.

- **Content and Document Management**
  Tools for securely creating, editing, sharing, and managing files—both within and across firewalls, as well as online and offline. Vendors that offer this type of cloud-based application include Dropbox; Agility; and Clickability.

- **Enterprise Resource Planning (ERP)**
  This category of application takes all information from all functions of a business—finance, human resources, manufacturing, distribution, and others—and brings it together into a single place to be analyzed. ERP had previously been outside the reach of smaller businesses, as products tended to be quite expensive, required technical specialists to customize, and were not terribly user-friendly. However, new cloud-based ERP systems are affordable, require minimal technical expertise to implement, and are infinitely easier to use. Vendors offering cloud-based ERP include SAP; NetSuite; and QAD.

- **Human Resources (HR)**
  These applications cover the gamut of activities related to hiring, compensating, managing, and terminating people. They include both payroll and the highly data- and processing-intensive tasks involved in benefits management. Vendors that provide these applications include Workday; Ultimate Software; Employease; and Intuit.

- **Inventory Management**
  These tools help you manage your supplies—raw materials and finished products—as well as vendors, your warehouse,

barcodes, transactions, and more. You can find applications in this category from Red Prairie; ClearSpider; and FishBowlInventory.

- **Personal Productivity**
  Any software that your employees use to manage routine, general business tasks. This includes word processing, spreadsheets, presentation, email, and similar applications. Typically, these applications are loaded onto each user's desktop independently, yet cloud versions of the most popular office productivity suites are increasingly available. Google; Zoho; and (soon) Microsoft all have offerings in this area.

- **Project Management**
  This fairly broad category overlaps with other types of cloud applications listed here. It includes everything from collaboration software for teams working on projects together, to scheduling applications, budget-tracking solutions, and applications that automate the administration and quality assurance aspects of taking projects to successful conclusions. Vendors offering cloud-based project management solutions include WorkZone; VisionProject; Accept360; and Basecamp.

- **Telephony**
  This category of cloud solutions is already saving small businesses considerable dollars. These services offer free or very-low-cost ways to leverage the Internet to make phone calls, send faxes, record conversations, hold multiparty conference calls, and more. Although early cloud-based telephony services suffered from quality issues, they're getting more business-appropriate every day. Vendors offering cloud-based telephony services include (of course) Skype; Callture; PenTerra Networks; and RingCentral.

- **Email Marketing and Marketing Automation**
  Vendors offering such cloud solutions include Marketo; Eloqua; Exact Target; Emma; Constant Contact; Vertical Response; Hubspot; and Silverpop.

- **E-commerce**
Some vendors are Netsuite; Intuit; Paypal; and Yahoo! Merchant.

Step Three: Do Your Homework

At this point you've identified business challenges that could be addressed by moving to the cloud, and found actual cloud solutions that claim to solve them. Now it's time to roll up your sleeves and get to work researching which solutions will best suit your particular business needs.

- **Run the numbers**
Go back to the preliminary financial worksheet you completed in Chapter 6 (page 86). Now that you've got actual product candidates, plug in the real numbers. Although you may generally choose to make business decisions on a more intuitive level, it's always a good idea to pencil out some ballpark figures of what things cost, and to quantify the benefits you expect to reap.

- **Read the reviews**
Happily, you have lots of support when it comes to evaluating the quality of the various options, since reviews of cloud applications are all over the Internet. Buyer beware, however: Not all reviews are created equal! Some are submitted by well-established "labs" (typically the research arms of respected industry magazines, newspapers, or websites that have established rigorous standards and methodologies for testing), while some are by individuals who may or may not possess any expertise. But don't discount user reviews altogether: Sometimes they provide much more insightful and realistic assessments of a cloud service—particularly if they're written by business users who have actually implemented the solution in real-world environments. Bugs and glitches that can escape the notice of a two-week laboratory simulation often reveal themselves when put in the hands of actual business users.

down-to-earth
ADVICE

"Evaluate a cloud provider the way you would a potential employee. Are they a good fit? It's not about whether the potential vendor is perfect: They won't be. It's about how they manage problems and if they operate in a way that's compatible with your business."

—Marnie Webb,
co-CEO of TechSoup

BEST REVIEW SITES FOR CLOUD APPLICATIONS

- CNET (http://www.cnet.com)
- INFOWORLD (http://www.infoworld.com)
- ZDLABS (http://oasis.peterlink.ru/~dap/nnres/misc/data/Benchmarks/12.html)
- GETAPP (http://www.getapp.com/)

- **Browse the vendor's support forums**
  You'd be amazed what you will glean from the questions and problems other customers are having with the solution.

- **Interview other customers**
  Never, *ever*, skip this step. No matter how pressed you are for time, and how impatient to get the solution implemented, always ask for customer references—ideally in your industry—and talk to a minimum of three of them. Of course, the cloud vendor will only give you the names of satisfied customers. Still, you'd be surprised at how candid and critical even the happiest customers can be. If possible, visit the customer site in person, and ask for a demonstration of how the customer uses the service. You'll gain a much better sense of whether it's a good fit for your particular employees and culture.

- **Check out the cloud vendor's history, reputation, and financial strength**
  As discussed in Chapter 4 (page 52), you don't want to sign up for a cloud service, implement it, migrate your data, reengineer your business processes, and train your users only to have the vendor close its doors or discontinue the service six or 12 months down the road. You want a vendor with the financial resources to continually improve and maintain the application and service. If a vendor is new to the cloud but is an otherwise established company, look at its overall reputation. Companies with reputations for excellence in one field are likely to maintain that excellence in the cloud. See page 54 on what data to look for when evaluating the finances of a cloud vendor, and where to find it.

checklist:

Questions to Ask Potential Cloud Service Providers

☐ Will I be able to add more users as needed? Is there any limit to the number of users I can have?

☐ Can I scale back the number of users if I need to at any time?

☐ Can your solution integrate with my other cloud solutions?

☐ Can your solution integrate with my current on-premise solutions?

☐ What is the minimum time commitment I must make to using your service?

☐ What type of service-level agreements (SLAs) do you offer?

☐ How many and what type of outages have you experienced in the last 12 months? If you had any, what was the problem? What have you done to ensure that it won't happen again?

☐ What sorts of customizing can I do to the service?

☐ If you have various "tiers" of service, what are the feature and price differences between them?

☐ What are the initial costs? What will it cost to turn on your service? To maintain it?

☐ How do you provide tech support? (24/7 phone support? An online knowledgebase? Tiered levels of paid support?) How do I get in touch with you in an emergency?

☐ What are your backup and disaster recovery plans?

☐ Do you have a presence in my industry? Do you know the challenges and difficulties I face in terms of rules and regulations? Can you give me references in my industry?

See checklist in *Chapter 5, page 71* for security questions to ask potential vendors.

- **Take a test drive**

  Many cloud service providers offer no-cost trials—typically, a 30-day use of the service for free. Take advantage of this. See whether the cloud application meets most of your business needs. Allow for a bit of time to get used to the "newness" of the application, watch a training video or two, and try to actually use the application to do your job. This will give you a good sense of its overall ease-of-use.

- **Consult your technology experts**

  Sooner or later—whether you have in-house IT gurus or use an external consulting firm—you'll want to bring your own experts into the evaluation process. Some small businesses will choose to do this upfront, perhaps even delegating the due diligence to their technology professionals. Others may wish to wait until they've made their final decision, and then will ask their technologists to validate their findings. Either way, keep your technologists in the loop.

- **Consult your users**

  Again, moving to the cloud can represent a big change for your employees, who are accustomed to a certain way of working. Ideally, users should be brought into the process very early on, as they can provide invaluable input on how to improve existing business processes. More on this in Chapter 8.

- **Plan for growth**

  Choose a provider you can grow with. When choosing particular solutions, keep in mind features you may not need now but will eventually require. Make sure your provider offers them.

worksheet:

Calculate Minimum Requirements

Use this worksheet to determine your needs for cloud solutions you are considering.

CLOUD SOLUTION UNDER CONSIDERATION		
Initial Number of Users		
Estimated Future Number of Users		
Other Cloud Solutions with Which It Must Integrate		
On-Premise Software with Which It Must Integrate		
"Must-Have" Features		
"Wish List" of Features		

Comparing Competing Cloud Solutions

Use this worksheet to compare the costs, reviews, and advantages and weaknesses of competing cloud solutions.

CLOUD SOLUTION UNDER CONSIDERATION		
Monthly Cost		
One-Time Fees		
What Other Customers Said		
What Reviews Said		
What My Users Say		
Unique Advantages		
Weaknesses		

Begin Formulating Your Cloud Strategy

Now you can begin to put together a tentative schedule and budget for moving to the cloud.

If yours is a new business, you may want to begin having cloud-based applications handle all or most of your business functions. That way, you won't have to face the difficulties involved in migrating data, integrating the new application with existing on-premise software, writing off the sunk costs in legacy systems, or persuading users that the new application will improve their lives. You only need to consider which functions, if any, you're not comfortable putting in the cloud at any time or whether there's mission-critical and industry-specific software that's not yet available in the cloud.

But if yours is an existing business, you'll want to approach your move-to-the-cloud strategy in a more measured fashion. Remember, transitioning to the cloud is a journey—you don't want to, or need to, move all your functions at once.

In determining which functions to move early on in your journey, keep in mind the following:

- **How discrete the function is**
  In other words, does it stand alone or is it significantly integrated with other applications or functions? You may want to dip your toe in the water with a seemingly discrete application. Expect, however, that as you discover the increased functionalities of cloud services, you may wish to integrate applications you once treated as discrete with other applications, either on-premise or in the cloud.

- **Need for remote access**
  Functions that require employees to work or to access data remotely are excellent candidates for early transition to the cloud. Since cloud-based data is available wherever there's an Internet connection, this gives you great flexibility. This is one of the reasons that CRM—sales force automation—has been one of the biggest early cloud successes.

"Do some customer sleuthing. When picking a cloud vendor, find people that are doing what you're doing. People are sharing. Read online reviews and customer satisfaction reports."

—Marnie Webb, co-CEO of TechSoup

factoid

In a 2011 Gartner survey of over 2,000 CIOs, respondents listed cloud computing as their number one priority.[2]

- **Time until next upgrade**
One of the great advantages of cloud-based applications is that you don't have the significant expense of software upgrades. As you face costly upgrades, you certainly want to look at cloud-based alternatives. That's the perfect time to switch, as you'll see immediate cost savings.

- **Need for collaboration**
Most cloud-based applications make it easier for people—employees, contractors, customers, vendors—to collaborate, whether onsite or offsite. Project-management and document-sharing tools are likely candidates for going to the cloud earlier rather than later.

- **Pressing need to reduce costs**
If you and your staff feel frustrated by the expense and wasted time of software or data that requires multiple entries and suffers from lack of both power and functionality, then (sooner rather than later) you might consider switching to cloud-based alternatives.

- **Need to catch up with competitors**
If you've fallen behind the curve and are losing out to your competitors, because you are saddled with old or outdated processes (especially because you couldn't afford the cost of upgrades or new hardware), improving your situation should be a critical consideration when looking at which cloud-based solutions to adopt early on.

Bottom line: There's no need to rush in your move to the cloud. Perhaps start with one application from a trustworthy source and buy one to five "seats." Get used to having your data and processes on and over the Internet rather than on-premises. It's likely that once you see the power, ease, and cost savings of cloud-based applications, you'll want to hurry up and move even *more* of your functions to the cloud.

2. "Gartner Executive Programs Worldwide Survey of More Than 2,000 CIOs Identifies Cloud Computing as Top Technology Priority for CIOs in 2011," Gartner, January 21, 2011, http://www.gartner.com/it/page.jsp?id=1526414.

worksheet:

Beginning to Plan

Use this worksheet to calculate costs and develop a timeline for implementing the cloud solutions you have chosen.

CLOUD SOLUTION CHOSEN				
Business Problem				
Total Implementation Cost (*see page 86*)				
Implementation Start Date				
Estimated Completion Date				
Notes				

Company:
PHONE WORKS

www.phoneworks.com

Cloud Service:
BUILDING NEXT-GENERATION
SALES ORGANIZATIONS

Insight provided by:
ANNEKE SELEY,
FOUNDER AND CEO

As experts in sales strategy, Phone Works helps businesses selling B2B and B2C build next-generation (Sales 2.0) sales organizations by assisting with the development and execution of cloud technology roadmaps that support metrics- and-data-driven sales function.

Q *What should businesses do now to prepare for a move to the cloud?*

A Analyze critical business functions such as account- ing, inventory control, sales, and marketing to identify those functional areas that will see the greatest impact while being the least disruptive. Start a small pilot with open-minded individuals in one part of the business. Learn from experiences and track results before rolling out to your entire organization.

Q *What's an unsung benefit of moving to the cloud?*

A The flexibility to buy products and services when and how you prefer. And the ease of evolving your systems, processes, and business strategies over time. Cloud tech- nologies also open up opportunities for expanded candi- date pools of remote and mobile workers and allow small and medium businesses to compete with much larger com- panies because they don't have to invest in expensive IT resources. Our company is a perfect example. We are a "vir- tual business" with consultants working from home offices and our clients' offices across the U.S., Canada, and Europe. Our systems are all cloud-based and we have no IT staff.

Q *What causes cloud hesitation and how do you address it?*

A While some companies lack an understanding of the value of cloud technologies, the most common reason we observe is one that is never cited: It's easier to continue doing what has become routine and normal. But the transformation of sales operations, supported by technology, leads to increased rev- enue, better financial results, and longer, tighter relationships with clients.

Q *What will a typical small or medium IT infrastructure look like in 10 years?*

A While our crystal ball is as cloudy as the next, we do expect a higher percentage (75–90 percent) of small and medium companies to migrate all their sales-related IT infrastructure to the cloud.

chapter

8

Ready, Set, Launch! Migrating to the Cloud

By the end of this chapter...

you'll have a working plan for beginning
your migration to the cloud.

Taking the Next Step

At this point, you've identified the business problem (or problems) you need to solve. You've researched which cloud solutions address these problems. You've done your due diligence on comparing the relative advantages and disadvantages of similar solutions—including the respective cost and benefits of each. And you've researched the cloud service providers you're considering to determine their financial stability, interviewed their customer references, read the reviews of their solutions, and taken test drives to get a hands-on feel for how the solutions work. You've even prepared a tentative plan that lays out which cloud solutions you plan to implement and in what time frame.

Now it's time to begin to apply what you've learned by actually migrating to your first cloud application.

Be Sensitive to the Difficulty of Change

Unless you've just opened your doors, you rarely have a blank slate opportunity in your business for installing an application. Even if you are automating a process that previously was done manually—that is, you're not replacing an existing piece of on-premise software, but are using cloud technology to streamline a task that was previously done using Word documents, Excel spreadsheets, or even paper—you can't treat lightly the change you're about to make. That's because you're asking your employees to learn a brand-new way of doing things, in addition to requiring them to learn a new technology.

In effect, your employees are hit with a double whammy: a new business *process,* and a new *tool* (the cloud application) that automates that process. They must master both, simultaneously, while continuing to get their jobs done.

Keep this in mind as you go through the steps and exercises recommended in this chapter. You're doing much more than simply introducing your employees to a new technology. You're ushering in a new way of working—so the organizational or cultural learning curve might end up being much tougher for your users than the technological one.

Your No. 1 Migration Priority: Ensure the "Cleanliness" of Your Data

Your ability to gain the most out of migrating to a new cloud-based application depends on one thing more than anything else: good data. The fact is, even if you and your employees have been extraordinarily careful about the accuracy of the

learn the lingo

DATA CLEANSING: Preparing your data for migration involves first cleansing it to ensure that it is accurate, complete, valid, consistent, uniform, and unique. The two-step process of cleansing involves detecting problems in the data and then fixing them.

DATA FIELDS: The categories in the application into which you put your data. Examples of data fields include product SKU, product size, product shipping weight, and product price.

information you've stored in your existing system—whether on-premise or cloud-based—you should double check the accuracy and completeness of that data before migrating it to the new one. Most applications that have been in use for any length of time contain errors. These errors can arise from simple typos made when someone sat down at a keyboard and entered data in a hurry; they can involve duplicate data—for example, you might have several accounts that were created for one customer; or they can be the result of corruption caused by a software glitch or virus.

Whatever the reason, you should perform what's called "data cleansing" before migrating any data. The data cleansing process involves two steps: first *detecting* problems, then fixing them.

down-to-earth
ADVICE

Don't move bad data from one application to another. It's worth the investment to cleanse your data before a migration.

"CLEAN DATA" HAS THESE CHARACTERISTICS:

- **It's accurate**
  The right data is in the right place—for example, your annual revenues are correctly recorded.

- **It's complete**
  You're not missing anything. For example, if you've been collecting the daily sales for each of your 10 retail clothing stores for the past five years, you want to make sure that you haven't failed to record the figures for any day or any store over that period.

- **It's valid**
  The data makes sense according to logical "constraints" on what you're trying to capture. For example, the hire dates of your employees must (obviously) be in the past. Likewise, if employees enter their daily hours into an application, they can't clock more than 24 hours in any given day.

- **It's consistent**
  One piece of data doesn't contradict another piece. For example, if you've sold 100 widgets in a given period, and each widget costs customers $100, then total revenues for that period can't be $500,000. That would be inconsistent.

- **It's uniform**

  All data is recorded in the same designated format. For example, all dates have been entered using the dd/mm/yyyy form.

- **It's unique**

  There's no duplicate data that could adversely affect the application.

  Data cleansing is a fairly specialized process. It's also time-consuming and expensive. Chances are you'll want to hire a third-party expert to do this. Is it worth it? For business-critical applications, absolutely. Think of the cost to your business if bad data causes you to underestimate a major bid for a large project. Or to consistently overpay taxes.

GARBAGE IN, GARBAGE OUT

The term "garbage in, garbage out" has been around from the early days of the computer industry, but it's more relevant now than ever. It states what should be the obvious: If what you put into a computer is nonsense (or erroneous), what will come out is also nonsense (or erroneous). Why isn't this always obvious? Probably because there's a certain mystique to an "answer" that's been provided by a computer—a sense that a black box crunching numbers and facts has more legitimacy than a human-generated opinion. Of course, that's silly. If you're attempting to calculate the profit margin on a widget you manufacture, and fail to capture all the costs—both direct and indirect—associated with manufacturing that widget, you'll end up with a "garbage" answer. Amusingly, a more updated version of this old programmers' mantra is "garbage in, gospel out," referring to the unearned trust that people place in computerized data.

Verifying and Mapping Data "Fields"

Data fields are simply the "blank spaces," or categories in applications, into which you enter data. For example, if you have a human resource (HR) application for collecting information about job candidates, you probably have a field for candidates' names, a field for their phone numbers, one for their social security numbers, and so on.

So, after cleansing your data, the second most important task in migration is figuring out how the fields in your existing application relate to those in your new application—for they're unlikely to align precisely. In some cases, you may want to eliminate certain fields because you realize that you rarely use the data stored in them. For example, you may have been asking candidates where they attended high school, and entering their answers in a "high school attended" field, yet never actually going back and looking at that field for any reason.

Alternatively, you may have realized that you haven't been collecting information that could be of great value to you. So when you migrate to the new cloud-based HR application, you want to create a new field for the number of years of education past 12th grade so you can track the correlation between your employees' job performance and advanced education.

Sometimes the new cloud-based application you're migrating to may simply call a field by a different name. You need to make sure that your old fields align correctly with the ones in the new application.

Your Migration Plan

Keeping in mind the dual nature of a cloud migration—both process *and* technological change—your plan for a successful one should include the following steps.

STEP 1: CREATE BUSINESS PROCESSES THAT STREAMLINE YOUR BUSINESS WHILE FULLY LEVERAGING THE CAPABILITIES OF THE CLOUD

You shouldn't blindly adjust the way you do business to suit how the cloud solution works. Conversely, unless you're entirely delighted with your current business processes—and see no room for improvement there—you shouldn't simply use the cloud solution to do things the way you've always done them. (Otherwise, ask yourself: Why change, if you're keeping things the same?) Take this migration as an opportunity to creatively work with your employees to consider ways in which the cloud can enable greater efficiency, productivity, and cost savings.

For instance, if you decide to move from a desktop sales tool to a cloud-based CRM application, suddenly you have all sorts of possibilities for enabling collaboration between employees who may never have talked to one another before.

factoid

In 1980, storage device maker Seagate introduced the first hard drive for microcomputers. It could store up to five megabytes of data. Today's entry-level laptops typically have more than a thousand times that capacity.

worksheet:

Your Existing and Future Data Fields

Use this worksheet to determine if and how the data fields in your existing application relate to your new application. Use the bottom portion to brainstorm on new fields that may be of use. Have handy some typical reports you run, to help you determine some of this information.

CURRENT FIELD	RETAIN OR ELIMINATE?	RENAME? IF YES, CHOOSE UPDATED NAME	FORMAT (E.G., MM/DD/YY; LAST NAME FIRST; NUMBERS IN 1,000s)	FIELDS FOR FUTURE NEEDS

NEW FIELD/TYPE OF INFORMATION	PURPOSE OF NEW FIELD	NAME OF NEW FIELD	FORMAT (E.G., MM/DD/YY; LAST NAME FIRST; NUMBERS IN 1,000s)	FIELDS FOR FUTURE NEEDS

Say a customer calls your service center with a question about one of your products. During the call, your service representative learns that this customer is considering switching vendors because of a low-bid offer from one of your competitors. Previously, that tidbit would have vanished once the service call ended. But with a cloud-based CRM, this information is immediately communicated to the sales team, giving you the opportunity to save the account.

A critical aspect of rethinking business processes is to identify where you currently have "disconnects"—points where important information needs to be manually taken from one application and manually keyed into another—and where it makes sense to integrate disparate applications together. (See Chapter 9 for more on integration.) For example, the manufacturing administrators who monitor your raw-materials database may currently need to pick up the phone and call procurement when supplies run low. A procurement staffer then must manually enter the order into the procurement system. Finally, when the supplies are received, that information needs to be communicated in reverse. With a cloud-based purchasing application that's integrated with the raw-materials database, all this happens automatically. No need for rekeying! Not only are the inevitable errors eliminated, but you free up time for employees who can focus on more important tasks.

STEP 2: CLEANSE THE DATA

As detailed above, make sure you have solid data that has been thoroughly vetted to ensure that it's accurate, complete, valid, consistent, uniform, and unique.

ANTICIPATE YOUR NEEDS

When determining which data fields you'll want to establish for your new cloud-based application, make sure you think ahead. You may only currently manufacture three products. But you anticipate that within five years you'll have expanded to 10 or more. Be sure you have adequate fields designated to capture the information you'll need at that point.

"Before you choose a cloud application, figure out what data you want, and what you can't do without. Ask yourself what your endgame is. Ask yourself how fast, and how big, you think you are going to grow. Make sure that the vendor doesn't constrain you in any way."

— Paul Leary, president, Blackbird Vineyards

STEP 3: DETERMINE WHICH FIELDS YOU NEED FOR THE NEW CLOUD-BASED APPLICATION

Look at the reports you typically run on your old application, and which data you routinely use. If no one is using the data from a particular field, eliminate the field. Now ask yourself whether you need any new fields—either now, or in the future. Use the worksheet on page 114 to help you sort this out.

STEP 4: PUT INTO PLACE INTEGRATION AND CONNECTORS TO OTHER APPLICATIONS

Now that you've identified what integrations you need, you have to find them. For connections between the most popular cloud business applications, integration technology like Dell Boomi can easily be deployed by nontechnical business users. For more specialized applications, or for cloud applications that have been heavily customized, you may need to hire a consultant to help. But due to the nature of the cloud, today even custom programming to integrate applications is both easier and faster—and therefore cheaper—to accomplish than by trying to integrate traditional on-premise solutions. Although on-premise applications have what are called "application programming interfaces" (APIs) that exist to tie them to other applications, they tend to be limited. Cloud-based APIs are much more open and flexible (after all, "open and flexible" is the SaaS mind-set).

STEP 5: MIGRATE DATA

The ETL (extract, transform, and load) part of moving data from an old to a new system is probably the most challenging aspect of migration. You may be lucky, and the data you've stored in your on-premise application may seamlessly flow into your cloud application. But chances are good that you'll need to do some fancy footwork. For starters, the cloud application you've chosen might have different categories of data than your original application did. For example, you may have been collecting only total sales in your point-of-sale system, whereas the new cloud-based application captures the specific product category or SKU. Or, if you're trying to migrate from a very old or highly customized system, you may not be able to extract the data at all. In such cases, as tedious and time-consuming as it might be, you may need to do a lot of manual chores. Allow yourself plenty of time to work out the kinks in the data migration.

QUICK TIP

Many cloud vendors will make it easy for you to migrate data, by providing what they call "front-end" interfaces to help you readily move data from certain popular applications—both on-premise and cloud—into theirs. If you think about this, it makes sense, as one of the biggest barriers to signing up new customers is that businesses worry about the time and expense of migrating data. For example, Salesforce CRM offers such an interface to businesses that have previously stored most customer data in ACT! or Excel.

STEP 6: TEST

By this time, your technology team should be involved, if they aren't already. You'll need their help testing that everything works as it should. They should pay particular attention to the integration points: Is data flowing from one application to another as designed? Is the data "clean" (free of errors) and complete (nothing truncated or missing)? Has the application been properly configured to fit your business's needs? You may wish to first test whether the migration has been successful on a small sample of data before migrating all the data over. That way, if there's a problem, you catch it early without having to redo the entire process.

STEP 7: TRAIN USERS

While cloud applications tend to be much easier to learn and use than their on-premise counterparts, keep in mind that users are learning new business processes at the same time they're learning about the new technology tool. You may want to take training in stages: First, introduce the tool, and allow users to log on and get their feet wet navigating around the various features. Second, introduce them to the new processes. Give them plenty of time to absorb and practice them—and assume that productivity will inevitably decline during the transition period. Finally, be prepared to follow up on any online or group training you do with one-on-one sessions with employees as necessary.

STEP 8: GO LIVE

Finally, the day arrives: You formally turn off the old application and switch to the cloud solution. Congratulations!

STEP 9: WORK OUT GLITCHES

But be prepared. Your migration isn't complete—not by a long shot. Ready yourself for a two-to-three-month period in which you'll be solving any number of problems that arise, both large and small. Keep your technologists on call—you'll probably need them. Many of the calls you get from users will likely be easily answered by your cloud vendor's support team. But some could require rethinking your initial configuration, or your new business process or information flow. Be prepared to be flexible during this transitional time. And keep in mind that a lot of these issues will be people related. For example, some users may balk at using the new system, or make so many errors that they need additional training. During this transition, don't be surprised at lower worker productivity, until your employees adjust to the new way of doing things.

STEP 10: SOLICIT AND IMPLEMENT IDEAS FOR IMPROVEMENT

After the first few months, things should calm down considerably. And if your experience mirrors that of early cloud users, it should be an extremely positive one. Still, make clear to your employees that you welcome their feedback on an ongoing basis. Encourage them to tell you how your business could leverage the cloud solution to even greater advantage. Ask them to brainstorm with each other on how to enhance business processes. And make sure that you communicate regularly with your cloud-service provider—which, in turn, depends on you to provide ideas on ways to improve its service.

Involve Employees Early in the Process

Even if you choose to limit the number of people involved in the upfront analysis and research of potential cloud solutions, at some point fairly early on you should invite participation from people who'll actually be using the new cloud service.

This is critical, for two reasons. First, one of the most common—and costliest—reasons that a company's technology investment can fail is that users refuse to adopt the new system. Change can be difficult even under the best conditions, and if workers feel that a new way of working is being thrust on them without their understanding how it benefits them, they can rebel.

Second, when it comes to understanding how best to perform their own jobs, your employees are the experts. And chances are good that you have certain employees who are exceptionally good at what they do. Tap into their expertise and leadership. Demonstrate to them the cloud applications you're considering. Ask them to work with you to design ways to make their jobs easier. Or ways in which the company, overall, could benefit from a cloud solution. Certainly, don't attempt to revamp an important business process without asking advice from the very people who will be expected to perform that new process day in and day out.

Of course, you should be open to the possibility that some employees will simply not like the idea of change, period. Even a new tool that makes their lives easier can seem threatening to them. So just because you get some pushback doesn't mean that your cloud migration strategy isn't the right direction for your business. *Do* be sensitive about the difficulty of change, and factor that into your migration strategy. Your transition to the cloud will go much more smoothly if you do so.

down-to-earth
ADVICE

"To help bring employees on board with the new process, identify an in-house go-to consultant. Not a technical expert, but a usage expert— someone that truly understands how the cloud solution makes the job easier and how it benefits the company."

—Marnie Webb, co-CEO, TechSoup

Company:
PRICELOCK

www.pricelock.com

Cloud Service:
ONLINE FUEL
PRICE PROTECTION

Insight provided by:
NAVEEN AGARWAL, CEO

Pricelock is the world's first company to offer online fuel protection to businesses of all sizes. Pricelock allows landscaping, construction, towing, distribution, and trucking companies to cap their gas or diesel cost and protect their bottom line.

CLOUD FILE: INSIDER INSIGHT

Q *What should businesses do now to prepare for a move to the cloud?*

A Examine your current products and processes to see which pieces can be easily isolated and componentized. Those components can then be independently validated in the cloud with minimal disruption to current operations.

Q *What's an unsung benefit of moving to the cloud?*

A The cloud enables you to offer services that simply could not be offered economically any other way.

Q *What will a typical small or medium IT infrastructure look like in 10 years?*

A Ten years from now, the typical IT infrastructure will primarily reside in the cloud. The initial cost of moving to the cloud will become small enough that starting new services on-premise will not be feasible for small and medium businesses.

Q *What causes cloud hesitation and how do you address it?*

A Companies often don't have the skill sets in-house to move to this new paradigm. Like many cloud-based solutions, Pricelock takes what could be very complex and makes it simple and easy to use. When small and medium businesses realize Pricelock is easy to use and drives business results with a positive impact on the bottom line, their hesitation begins to fade.

Integration: Sharing Data to Increase Business Intelligence

By the end of this chapter...

you'll understand what integration is, appreciate why it's important, and know how to begin doing it.

An Integration Strategy Is Vital to Success

For all the many benefits that the cloud offers small and medium businesses, SaaS applications have even greater power when they work with other business processes, not as standalone solutions. For businesses to truly embrace the cloud, they need to be able to share data between applications—whether in the cloud or on premise. Without this ability, cloud applications often are isolated "islands" of data, in effect harking back to the early days of business computing, when data was virtually locked up in huge, monolithic, mainframe computers, inaccessible to all but a privileged few.

The ability to *integrate* cloud applications with each other, and with traditional on-premise software, as well as with data from the Internet, is what makes the cloud a long-term solution with such exciting possibilities for small and medium businesses.

What Is Integration?

Integration is, at its most basic level, simply the ability to tie two or more disparate systems together so that data can flow easily from one to another.

For example, with the right integration plan, transactional information recorded in your cloud-based Salesforce CRM application can be automatically added to your on-premise QuickBooks financial records. Or, customer support issues documented in the CRM application can be made visible to your accounts receivable department—so everyone on your team can help keep customers happy.

Integration solutions synchronize data between applications and services, meaning that when something is updated in one system, it's automatically propagated in the connected systems.

Integration Works across a Variety of Applications

Integration. It's nothing new. Over the years, an entire industry of specialists and tools has flourished by doing nothing but tying together different computer systems for businesses. Yet the cloud era has ushered in a new set of integration challenges, both technical and organizational.

Today, to make your employees as productive as possible and to optimize your ability to seize business opportunities as they arise, you need to share data across *all* applications, whether they reside on users' desktop PCs, on a shared office server, or in the cloud. And, users need access to *all* types of applications from an increasingly diverse set of devices—

learn the lingo

CONNECTORS: These send and receive information to and from applications or data sources. By "connecting" to on-premise or cloud-based applications, connectors enable communication and integration between disparate sources of information.

DATA SILOS: Distinct databases of information that don't communicate with one another. Extracting and sharing data from a silo can be extremely difficult and time-consuming.

desktop PCs, laptops, smartphones, tablet computers, and whatever tomorrow brings—from anywhere in the world, at any time.

Integration Examples

APPLICATIONS TO INTEGRATE	BENEFIT
Sales + Finance	Share real-time quotes across teams; automate orders and invoices; reduce manual data reentry; enable sales team to see profit margins on specific customer accounts or deals; get immediate updates on sales transactions to finance department
Sales + Marketing + Finance	Track real-time results of marketing campaigns on actual sales; learn ROI of marketing campaigns
Sales + Finished Goods Inventory + Raw Goods Inventory	Ensure that your company can always fill orders; avoid having too much cash invested in raw materials and finished goods

A well-planned integration strategy will share data and intelligence across a variety of sources, including:

- **Packaged applications**
  Word processing, spreadsheet, or project management applications that reside on individual PCs or laptops. In the past, data created in these applications was generally stored on the individual machines and shared only via email or as a printout.

- **Server applications**
  Software stored on a separate machine or a server and shared by everyone over a local network designed in-house. Traditionally, if employees needed to get into this type of application from outside the building, they used a virtual private network (VPN) that they tapped into using the Internet.

- **Cloud applications**
  The newest type of software in the mix, cloud applications reside in remote locations and eliminate the need for packaged software and servers in the office. These applications are accessed via the Internet.

- **Data from external sources**
  Any outside information that helps employees do their job more effectively, such as information from the Internet; market research reports; or applications like Jigsaw, D&B, and OneSource that augment the data you have.

Today, companies are adopting multiple SaaS applications—not just one or two. *And* they want to integrate these with their existing resources. But traditional integration solutions weren't designed to deal with this volume or complexity. Happily, a number of impressive solutions have appeared on the market to address this.

You have three basic choices for how you will integrate your cloud applications with other applications. First, you can use your cloud service provider's application programming interface (API) to build a custom integration solution for your specific applications and needs. Second, you can hire a third-party consultant or systems integrator to build connections for you. Or, third, you can subscribe to a cloud-based integration solution.

The Benefits of Cloud-Based Integration

Cloud-based integration services are attractive for many of the same reasons that cloud-based applications are. They're flexible, cost-effective (when compared to on-premise solutions), and scalable. These include Layer7tech, Pervasive, Cast Iron Systems, and, in particular Boomi, which was acquired by Dell, and is reaping *rave reviews* from customers.

http://www.boomi.com/customers

- **User-friendly**
  Boomi boasts a drag-and-drop interface (see image on page 125) that enables users with minimal technical training to successfully integrate applications—no coding required. Prebuilt connectors for common integration needs, plus the ability to identify and create custom connections, make it relatively easy to build an integration solution that previously would have required months of custom programming by technical experts.

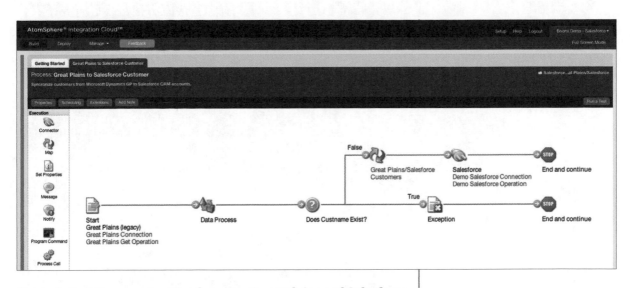

figure 1: Building a connection between Great Plains and Salesforce to share key customer information requires no coding experience. Dell Boomi provides step-by-step guidance to connect any combination of cloud and on-premise applications.

figure 2: To map data between connected applications in Boomi, simply drag a line from one application to the corresponding field of the second application.

NO MORE BLOOD, SWEAT, AND EXCEL! CREATING A SALES REPORT—BEFORE AND AFTER INTEGRATION

BEFORE INTEGRATION: Samantha's quarterly sales report is due Monday morning. She's spent all weekend exporting data from the sales and finance applications, gathering info on current deals from her team, and merging and massaging the data until it makes sense. The resulting Excel file is enormous. And something still isn't adding up right. She spent the last three hours fixing a recursive formula so that her pivot tables work correctly. Now she's dreading reformatting all the tables and charts. This is such a pain that Samantha's relieved she only has to do it four times a year. (Although, she has to admit, the arduous exercise provides the visibility she needs into how her team is doing.)

AFTER INTEGRATION: No matter the quarter, day, or time, Samantha can check the performance of her sales organization and make real-time adjustments to improve results. The integration solution gathers together all the data from different applications, after which the analytics package runs the numbers and automatically creates the reports, tables, graphs, and charts that Samantha and her CEO want to get their hands on.

- **Affordable**

  Like most cloud applications, you pay for what you need, when you need it. And if, like many small businesses, you don't have a large internal IT staff—or any such staff at all—you'll find that ease of use translates into money saved on planning, implementation, and maintenance of these solutions.

- **Flexible and scalable**

  A good cloud integration tool should be simple and flexible enough to be "productized" and used over and over within your business. So, instead of custom development for each new connection, you can repeatedly deploy what's already working, with minor modifications.

A robust cloud integration program will also be able to accommodate the fluid nature of cloud applications. Given that cloud service providers are continuously enhancing their offerings, your integration solution will need to adapt as your connected applications change.

TOP 5 REASONS TO TAKE ADVANTAGE OF INTEGRATION

So you've decided to move to the cloud. You'll find it pays to set aside time and money to develop a strategic integration plan. Using integration solutions, your company will:

1. SAVE TIME. Automatic data sharing replaces manual data entry. If someone is currently spending time finding data in one application, only to enter it into another application (for example, moving new customer contact info from your sales application to your financial package so an invoice can be prepared), it's time for integration.

2. REDUCE ERRORS. When you eliminate manual data entry and manual development of analytical spreadsheets and reports, you'll increase accuracy rates. If it was entered right the first time, it's automatically right everywhere it needs to be.

3. ELIMINATE "DATA SILOS." Take sales, for example: Lots of information in your CRM application has an impact on decisions outside of sales—marketing, finance, inventory management, and customer service, among others. An integration strategy will automate the process for sharing relevant data with the right applications.

4. INCREASE COMMUNICATION ACROSS TEAMS. It's always helpful when the right hand knows what the left is doing. When you share selected data across applications and departments, employees company-wide can keep an eye on the big picture.

5. IMPROVE RESULTS WITH "EVERYDAY ANALYTICS." Once data is automatically shared, it's easy to generate key reports—every day, if you want to. Think of it this way: If you were formerly checking performance reports quarterly, and you start looking weekly, that's 48 more opportunities every year to fine-tune your business strategy.

- **Global**
  If your business is geographically dispersed—as many small and medium businesses are these days—with "virtual" employees living across the country from each other,

or even on the other side of the world, cloud-based integration applications like Dell Boomi can be used in any number of different locations and still be centrally managed with an easy-to-use executive dashboard (accessed via the web, of course).

Given that, increasingly, individual departments and workgroups are purchasing their own cloud-based applications—in some cases, going a bit rogue because of their impatience with on-premise solutions—a solution like Boomi gives you, as owner or manager of your small business, a big-picture view of *all* the applications being deployed within your organization.

Planning Your Integration Strategy

You want your SaaS CRM solution to connect directly to your on-premise accounting software. You also want to link up your cloud-based email marketing campaign service to the CRM application. And then there's your point-of-sale system, which must feed into all these applications.

While it's important to consider business processes and plan ways to operate more efficiently so as to take advantage of easy access to analytical data, there's a lot more to think about when planning your integration strategy. The right strategy for you depends on a number of factors specific to your business. You should ask yourself these questions when making your decision:

- **Will my integration solution scale as I need it to?**
  It's critical that whatever integration solution you choose can grow as you do. And "growth" can mean a lot of things: Can your solution accommodate the number of users you anticipate having in, say, five years? Can it be deployed if you open a number of geographically dispersed offices? Can your integration solution handle a growing number of applications in your software portfolio? Does it have the capability to process the volume of data you're likely to accumulate in both the near- and long-term?

1. "2010 Digital Universe Study," GigaOM, April 26, 2010, http://gigaom.files. wordpress.com/2010/05/2010-digital-universe-iview_5-4-10.pdf.

- **Do I have sufficient personnel with the right skills to implement and maintain this solution?**
  This is a critical question. Building integration between systems requires skill and time. After the solution has been built, it must be maintained. And if any of the applications change—which is a virtual certainty when dealing with cloud applications—you need to possess the resources to keep the integration current, as well.

- **How much am I willing to pay for integration?**
  Since few small businesses have the personnel in-house to do custom programming, pursuing a custom-built strategy usually involves hiring a third-party systems integrator—and is usually accompanied by a huge bill. Do a comparison of commissioning a custom development project versus using a cloud-based integration solution. You may still need to hire outside help with the latter, but it will be a lot less expensive than the wholly custom programming route.

- **Will the integration solution work with all my applications and systems?**
  Not all integration solutions are created equal. Some will only work with a prescribed set of applications. Some won't cross the border between cloud and on-premise technologies. And you need to look ahead. What are your plans for deploying future applications? Is there anything about an integration strategy that would preclude you from implementing the exact solution you want sometime down the road?

CHOOSING A THIRD-PARTY INTEGRATOR

If you decide to use a third-party or independent systems integrator to help you bring together your cloud applications, make sure that you hire one that has actual hands-on cloud experience. Even dozens of years of experience in traditional software integration won't translate to success in the cloud. Luckily, most systems integrators understand that the cloud is the future, and have invested in developing cloud expertise.

The Value of Excellence™

Campos is especially appreciative of the analytics and reporting capabilities of the application. "Our management team uses the dashboard to check on such things as how many new case referrals we've received in a given day, week, or month," she said. "They can then drill down and see which nurses were assigned to each referral, and how many hours each of them worked...It would have been very difficult to calculate these things using our old manual system," Campos said.

ISYS
Diane Campos, General Manager

BACKGROUND
ISYS is a 14-year-old medical case management firm serving workers' compensation insurance companies and administrators. With more than 60 nurses employed as case managers in California, Nevada, and Arizona, ISYS helps streamline services and care for injured workers. ISYS professionals coordinate doctor appointments for patients; attend the appointments, as well as accompany the patients to any physical therapy or other outpatient services; provide their professional opinions of the quality of care the patient is receiving; and in general work closely with healthcare providers and insurance companies alike to help injured employees return to health and work as soon as possible.

CHALLENGE
Until four years ago, ISYS used a standalone, on-premise, PC-based application called CaseTracker to record the hours that field nurses worked and the tasks they completed. Nurses would keep track of what they did and how long it took, using any method that suited them, such as jotting down information in a traditional paper notebook, for example. They would then input this information into a Microsoft Word document and email it to the ISYS home office, where an administrator would print it out and then enter it into the system, using the CaseTracker software. From CaseTracker, ISYS could then calculate what each customer owed for services that ISYS workers had performed.

But the work didn't end there—the customer still required an invoice. To generate that, an ISYS administrator would print out a CaseTracker report that itemized the charges, and manually enter them into the on-premise accounting application, QuickBooks. Only then could an invoice be generated.

If a customer ever had a question about an invoice, ISYS would have to first consult QuickBooks, then look up the details of the account activity in CaseTracker—or, in some cases, call or email the field nurse for details. All this was very time-consuming and prone to errors.

"We were rapidly expanding, which was a positive thing, but the process for invoicing customers was cumbersome and costly because it required so much personnel time," said Diane Campos, general manager of managed care services at ISYS. "We needed to make a change."

SOLUTION
At the end of 2008, Campos approached salesforce.com with a list of questions. Could its cloud-based CRM application meet the needs of ISYS? Even though the ISYS invoicing process didn't fit into a tradi-

tional sales, marketing, or customer service category, Campos was very much interested in what she had heard about the solution, and hoped it could be customized to meet her needs.

"We definitely wanted a web application that was flexible enough to capture our nurses' time and activities and track by customer account," she continued. "Salesforce.com listened to us describe our dream application, and said we could easily build a customized application that would precisely meet our requirements."

So far, so good. Still, Campos wanted to push the envelope further by integrating the Salesforce application into QuickBooks, thus automating the invoicing process from start to finish. "That's when we heard about Boomi," she said. "Knowing that an integration tool existed that could do what we wanted was a big plus." Salesforce.com referred Campos to a strategic consulting partner that provided programming and program management services to build the application and Boomi integration links. The project was successfully completed in 2009.

BENEFITS

Today, ISYS nurses in the field log on to Salesforce from wherever they're working, and enter their hours and activity logs in seconds. That data is received by the ISYS home office instantaneously. The nurses love it, as it saves them considerable time and trouble, and lets them focus on their main jobs—caring for patients—rather than on paperwork.

Although ISYS has yet to do a formal ROI, Campos says, "We estimate that we have saved what it would cost to have hired another fulltime person and another halftime person. Given that an administrator would be paid $35,000 or $40,000 plus benefits, that's a substantial annual savings."

There's also the fact that automating the entire end-to-end process has eliminated the human errors that inevitably occur in a manual process, she said. And the application has proven highly reliable: In the two years since deploying the application, ISYS has had zero downtime.

Campos is especially appreciative of the analytics and reporting capabilities of the application. "Our management team uses the dashboard to check on such things as how many new case referrals we've received in a given day, week, or month," she said. "They can then drill down and see which nurses were assigned to each referral, and how many hours each of them worked."

Information like this can help ISYS understand whether it needs to hire more nurses for a particular city or geographic region, or whether certain nurses are being stretched too far with too many cases. "It would have been very difficult to calculate these things using our old manual system," Campos said. ■

CLARIFY YOUR CLOUD INTEGRATION NEEDS

No single approach is a perfect fit for all scenarios. The right approach for any company will depend on some of the following factors:

1. **RESOURCES:** Who will build your integration solutions? In-house resources, or the application administrator/business analyst, or both?

2. **PROJECT SCOPE:** How complex is the project? Is it a pilot project, a small departmental project, or a strategic company-wide deployment?

3. **BUDGET:** Does the integration portion of your cloud strategy have a sufficient budget?

4. **MAINTENANCE:** Who will help you adjust the integration as needs change and applications are updated?

- **Does the integration solution support processes that optimize my business's efficiency and profitability?** Moving to the cloud and integrating applications involves more than mere technology. In many cases, you'll also be rethinking and reengineering business processes. You therefore need to choose an integration solution that offers you quick, easy ways to automate common business process activities, like moving documents from one employee to another in a specific sequence and verifying that the data being used in the processes is "clean."

worksheet:

Your Integration Needs

BUSINESS GOAL	APPLICATIONS CONTAINING RELEVANT DATA (LIST ALL)	PLATFORM OF EACH APPLICATION (CLOUD, SaaS, ON-PREMISE, PC-BASED)	CURRENT BUSINESS PROCESS FOR RETRIEVING NECESSARY DATA	DESIRED BUSINESS PROCESS FOR RETRIEVING NECESSARY DATA	FREQUENCY/ SPEED WITH WHICH DATA NEEDS TO BE RETRIEVED

Company:
TALEO CORPORATION
www.taleo.com

Cloud Service:
TALENT MANAGEMENT

Insight provided by:
MICHAEL RADOVANCEVICH,
VICE PRESIDENT AND
CHIEF TECHNICAL OFFICER

Taleo is a cloud-based service that helps small businesses optimize all four pillars of talent management—recruiting, performance management, learning, and compensation—to improve organizational performance by unlocking the power of their people.

Q *What's an unsung benefit of moving to the cloud?*

A SaaS solutions allow small and medium businesses to focus on the core business, not on building up important but general corporate infrastructure. Cloud computing also allows small businesses to cost-effectively take advantage of sophisticated features and best practices that were once only available with significant IT investment.

Q *What causes cloud hesitation and how do you address it?*

A Confusion hinders adoption: confusion about what cloud computing and SaaS are, and what cloud technology can do. With cloud- or SaaS-based services, small businesses reap the benefits of not having to deploy a physical infrastructure like file and email servers, storage systems, or shrink-wrapped software. This means less time and money spent managing technology, and more time spent focusing on core business. Plus, the "anywhere, anytime" availability of cloud solutions means hassle-free collaboration between business partners and employees by simply using an Internet browser.

Q *What should businesses do now to prepare for a move to the cloud?*

A First, determine if the application you're considering supports core business processes and user requirements. Second, have a well-thought-out strategy for integrating data between new cloud-based solutions and existing applications, to avoid creating silos of inconsistent data. Third, focus on user needs because that really helps ensure adoption. Configuring your software to align with existing processes and user expectations makes the time-to-value even shorter than anticipated.

Q *What's your favorite customer success story?*

A Analysys Mason is a strategy and research consultancy focused on telecommunications, technology, and media. Thanks to the cloud's flexibility, within a week of being operational, the Taleo solution generated savings that paid for the entire cost of implementation. A year later, Analysys Mason estimates that it paid for Taleo for the next 10 years. Plus, with improved recruiting processes, agency use is down to 30 percent from 80 percent.

Analytics:
Using Data to Improve
Your Bottom Line

By the end of this chapter...

you'll understand how the cloud enables you to harness
and analyze business information in order to seize business
opportunities that give you a competitive advantage.

Transparency Means More Access to Information

The cloud enables transparency in business. And transparency, in turn,
enables accountability. Managers don't just get a phone call or email when
a salesperson has closed a deal. They see everything their sales professionals have done in every customer account—from initial cold calls, to product demos, to processing P.O.'s. Your marketing team can track how many
responses were received as a result of a particular email campaign—and you
can compare the results to the budget to decide whether the campaign was a
cost-effective one. Even your customers can follow the progress of a project
you're working on for them, provided you offer them a seat in the cloud. With
greater visibility, everyone has the ability to be on the same page, and to agree
collaboratively on what needs to be done next.

Yet transparency by itself isn't enough. It's one thing to have access to all
this information. It's another thing to make sense of it. That's where analytics
come in.

Analytics: The Biggest Hidden Advantage of the Cloud

A volatile business environment, economic uncertainty, and the continuous stream of new technological developments can all make it challenging to understand the right way to turn. And frequently you're being asked to turn on a dime. Analytics offer you quick but deep insight into your business that allows you to make these kinds of turns.

At the most basic level, analytics simply means applying computing power to analyze information. Analytics tools, however, are far more advanced and capable of more complex analyses than the basic reports you're used to extracting from spreadsheets or databases. They typically involve sophisticated statistical modeling and computational algorithms—and previously were too expensive for small- or medium-size businesses. The cloud has now leveled the playing field.

Cloud-based analytics applications enable you to do such things as track which geographic sales regions and products are performing well (or not); know which customers are likely to respond to a coupon in the Sunday paper, and which to an online ad on a popular website; and predict the corner of your city your target customers are most likely to visit if you opened a storefront there. You can then use all this insight to make decisions based on fact. Best of all, you don't have to perform any manual extraction, possess advanced technology skills, or earn a Ph.D. in statistics. Just pull your data from various systems into an analytics application, and it can generate detailed reports and graphics in real time.

The Power of Combining Cloud Integration with Cloud-Based Analytics

Having a way to integrate your cloud applications with each other, as well as with on-premise applications, is critical to getting the most out of the new analytics applications that are now available. (For details on integration, see Chapter 9.)

If you did not have the ability to integrate systems, here's what you would have to go through. Suppose you want to

BUSINESS INTELLIGENCE: The process of extracting and analyzing raw data in order to make informed business decisions. Although business intelligence was once a function solely of large enterprises, today small and medium-size businesses can conduct business intelligence easily and affordably. Tools such as integrators enable these smaller companies to pull data from disparate applications and plug it into an analytics application.

REAL-TIME DATA: Updates to the data that occur instantaneously. For example, when a salesperson closes a sale and enters it into a CRM, the information—contact name, order number, delivery information, and so forth—appears immediately in sales reports that others with access to the CRM can then use.

understand how much it costs you to cold-call 100 customers. You use a cloud-based CRM system that tracks the number and duration of calls made by each member of your telemarketing team. You also use on-premise financial software that contains all employee compensation data. To get the information you wanted, you'd first go to your CRM to extract all data about calls. Then you'd go to your financial application to extract the compensation data for each telemarketing associate. After entering all this information into a spreadsheet—manually, of course—you could eventually work out some numbers and then go to your presentation application and create some graphs. But this is hugely time-intensive. Few small businesses have the time or expertise to make full use of all the rich data they're collecting day in and day out. Then there's the niggling fact that all this manual extraction and rekeying of data is prone to errors.

Now look at what happens when you've integrated your applications using an integration platform like Dell Boomi. Boomi connects the applications you choose. You then use an analytics solution to analyze the data from these different applications. Data from disparate sources that you used to wrestle into Excel is now seamlessly accessible from a single screen. Now, you can get the cost per 100 calls in mere seconds. Then, in another few seconds, you calculate how much revenue you gain per 100 calls, and determine whether a cold-calling campaign is worth the investment. You can also see which of your telemarketers are the most successful—and whether you're paying them appropriately.

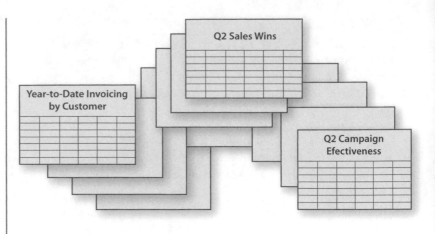

figure 1: Before integration and analytics: Information must be brought together from disparate applications, massaged, and then graphed to get an overall view of the business.

Application Integration

figure 2: After integration and analytics: Users can look at charts based on current data, drill down to investigate anomalies, and view historical trends and tracking.

Snapshot Metrics

checklist:

Data to Analyze

What data are you not analyzing in-depth now that could be more helpful? Check all that apply. If some areas that would benefit you aren't listed, add them at the bottom.

☐ Marketing

☐ Sales

☐ Customer service

☐ Customer retention

☐ Customer demographics, lifestyle, buying habits, and the like

☐ Trend monitoring

☐ Human resources

☐ Productivity

☐ Financial

☐ Supply chain

☐ Other: _____

☐ Other: _____

☐ Other: _____

☐ Other: _____

☐ Other: _____

☐ Other: _____

☐ Other: _____

COLLABORATIVE ANALYTICS

Before you analyze your data, you may need input from different departments in your organization. This is just one more task that highlights the benefits of the collaborative nature of the cloud. Other members of the team can add their input to the data, see what the analysis turns up, view reports and, most important—take action immediately. And along the way, everyone feels like a vital member of the team.

Your Analytics Plan

If your business is like most small businesses, you probably have collected more information than you know what to do with. You likely sense that some of this information contains valuable nuggets of insight. But how to begin mining them? Here's some advice.

- **Measure what counts**
  All too often, companies measure what's easiest to measure. For instance, how many hours did stockroom employees clock in last month? What were the annual revenues of each salesperson? But this doesn't mean these things are the right things to be looking at, if you want to maximize business success. With the help of integration, analytics changes everything. Instead of simply adding up hours of workers, also grab data from the raw goods inventory database and from the ERP system to determine if you're purchasing the right amounts of raw goods, and whether the process for procuring, receiving, and stocking those goods could be made more efficient and improve profit margins. Instead of merely rewarding the salesperson with the most revenues, pay attention to which salespeople are closing the highest percentage of deals. Or which ones are operating so efficiently and keeping costs so low that they're making the company more money than the so-called highest producers.

HOW TO IMPROVE YOUR BUSINESS PERFORMANCE WITH ANALYTICS

- **Measure what counts**
- **Perform regular reviews**
- **Focus on low-performing areas**
- **Get the right information to the right people**
- **Tweak your analytics strategy as necessary**

worksheet:

What Data Do You Need?

Fill out this worksheet to help you determine what types of data you'll need to address a specific problem in your business. Use the middle column as an example.

PROBLEM	DROP IN REVENUE LAST QUARTER	
Analysis to run	Revenue by: salesperson, region, store, product, customer, etc.	
Locations of various data	On-premise accounting application, cloud-based CRM, inventory management	
What emerged	Drop in traffic sources to website	
How can the problem be addressed?	Improve SEO and SEM; test banner ads; run analytics more frequently	
What other observations did you make that need to be investigated?	Revenue by product revealed 8% increase last quarter of mid-priced widgets—increase supply of raw materials to meet demand; revenue shrinking on ACME account	

B L A C K B I R D
V I N E Y A R D S

"Most California winemakers are small businesses. There's a gap in understanding best marketing practices. The big companies, the Amazons and Apples, are investing in systems that make ordering and fulfillment easier and more efficient. Smaller businesses haven't had the opportunity. But the cloud and integration tools like Boomi are changing that," he said.

Blackbird Vineyards
Paul Leary, President

BACKGROUND

Blackbird Vineyard has for more than a dozen years provided grapes to the best winemakers in California's Napa Valley. When Michael Polenske bought the vineyard in 2003, he expanded the business and began making his own premium label wines. From the beginning of this new undertaking, Blackbird wines received high praise: The first bottling was awarded 98 out of a possible 100 points by fine wine retailer Vinfolio, and was dubbed "the best Merlot nobody had ever heard of." Since then, Blackbird has become one of the most renowned wineries in the country. It sells its wines through both direct and wholesale distribution channels.

In 2008, Blackbird extended its brand with an innovative project, spearheaded by President Paul Leary, called Ma(i)sonry Napa Valley. This is an art, wine, and design collective created to draw visitors and tourists to the valley. It sells furnishings, fashion, and art created by globally recognized artists; acts as a venue for private events; and boasts a tasting room for Blackbird Vineyards' wines.

CHALLENGE

Before joining Blackbird in 2006, Leary spent 13 years at Duckhorn Wine Co., also in Napa, where he was vice president of sales and marketing. It was at Duckhorn that he developed his deep understanding of how emerging web-based technology could be applied specifically to the wine business. When he arrived at Duckhorn, its web presence consisted of three pages that did little but offer visitors a PDF brochure to download and fields to enter their names and contact information to get more information by mail. Within 12 months, Leary had replaced it with an ecommerce site that brought in $4 million in the first year alone. He then turned his attention to replacing an antiquated PC-based sales and marketing software application with one that would "get all business decision-makers on the same page." He had the satisfaction of seeing that in place before moving to Blackbird.

On joining Blackbird, Leary immediately began applying all he'd learned at his previous job to the new business. He had a significant advantage, since he was working with a green field as far as technology went. The owner, Michael Polenske, had done little but create a stand-alone ACT! database to hold his contacts. Leary's first decision: to investigate cloud-based applications.

"For our main sales and marketing database," said Leary, "I knew I needed a user-friendly system that was multiuser—not sitting on someone's laptop or desktop—and collaborative: something that promoted communication between all employees, because the data was easily accessible from anywhere."

SOLUTION

Leary's first step was to deploy Salesforce CRM. "Salesforce. com has a very flexible structure that didn't require us to go through a massive design phase to create a system that met our needs," he said. He hired San Francisco–based consulting firm, Hisoft, a specialist in Salesforce, to migrate the data that had been in the ACT database.

That accomplished, Leary implemented an ecommerce application for the Blackbird website, and also, when Ma(i)sonry opened its doors, a client-server–based point-of-sale application to handle on-premise sales.

But while he was happy with the individual applications, Leary wasn't satisfied that each one represented a different little "island" of information. To implement his ambitious marketing plans, he needed to be able to easily combine data from all of them. He turned to Dell Boomi. With the help of Hisoft, he was able to integrate the totality of his cloud-based and on-premise applications together and to access the data from a single dashboard.

BENEFITS

Today, Leary has a wealth of important business information at his fingertips—and the ability to slice and dice it so that he gets valuable insight into Blackbird's operations. He can see which customers purchase wine online from the company website, which ones shop at the Ma(i)sonry premises, and which ones buy through both channels.

"First and foremost," Leary asked, "are our customers crossing between our two brands? If so, how do they first hear about us? What encourages them to buy more? Do they respond better to marketing emails or traditional mailers? We can now answer all those questions, and more."

So deep is his knowledge of customer behavior that Leary can now do precise segmentation. "Most businesses our size don't have this capability," he said. "They may have a web-based shopping cart, and a CRM application, but that's it. We have total insight into every channel we have—from wholesale, to export, to private-client direct, to strategic business partner. Without this kind of visibility, we wouldn't be as successful as we've been at growing sales through demand-generation marketing activities.

"Most California winemakers are small businesses. There's a gap in understanding best marketing practices. The big companies, the Amazons and Apples, are investing in systems that make ordering and fulfillment easier and more efficient. Smaller businesses haven't had the opportunity. But the cloud and integration tools like Boomi are changing that," he said. ■

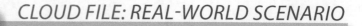

CLOTHING MANUFACTURER AND RETAILER:
You're a designer and manufacturer of high-end clothing. To capture customer data and share it across applications, you decided to integrate a cloud-based CRM with your existing shopping cart and point-of-sale (POS) software. Now you're ready to launch your first marketing campaign in which you'll analyze data from these combined systems. In the past, you waited until campaigns were finished before reviewing them and determining what worked, and what didn't. Any lessons learned would be incorporated into subsequent campaigns. This time, though, you can optimize the campaign in real time. The first campaign launched with the integrated applications involves sending out a mix of email and online ads. After the first few days, it's obvious the email has problems: The response rate is dismal. By doing some internal testing, you realize that a poorly worded discount offer is causing the email to go straight to your potential customers' spam in-boxes. You fix that, and your response rate goes through the roof. In the meantime, the online ads are doing so well that you double the frequency.

In addition to measuring your marketing campaigns, you've also begun to measure productivity in your manufacturing process on a weekly basis. After looking at the analytics, you realize that productivity has suddenly slowed by 6 percent on your flagship product: a line of designer jeans. You're able to quickly pinpoint the problem to malfunctioning cutting equipment. Had you checked productivity only at the end of the month—or worse, quarterly—you wouldn't have noticed until a significant amount of damage had been done to your bottom line.

SALES:

You recently integrated your CRM and financial software to measure costs per call and revenue by sales rep, as discussed earlier (pages 136-137). By analyzing all this data together, you discover that three of your 12 sales reps are doing much worse than average in terms of profitable deals—even though those three had impressive overall revenue numbers. You realize that some of those whom you consider your best salespeople are racking up huge expenses in pursuing deals that ultimately don't yield a sufficient amount of profit to justify the expenses. By providing the sales team with feedback on their profit margins, as well as their overall sales figures, you're able to improve the overall profitability of the firm.

- **Perform regular reviews**

  Every time you measure anything about your business (such as sales volume, customer service satisfaction, profit margins, or inventory turns), you have a chance to give feedback to your workers that will help them do their jobs better. So collect as much data as is feasible, and then analyze it regularly and often. Otherwise, by the time you realize you have a problem, it may be too late to solve it.

  Suppose you analyze sales information at the end of every quarter. If sales in your Texas region plummeted at the beginning of the quarter, you wouldn't know until almost three months later. Something that would have been relatively simple to fix—you had unfortunately hired a less-than-diplomatic receptionist at the regional service center—by then had lost you a significant number of customers.

  When you analyze your data quarterly, you have only four opportunities per year to act. If, by contrast, you analyze your data monthly, you have 12 chances to take action. Do it weekly and you have 52 opportunities to steer your company in the right direction.

factoid

According to Gartner, more than a third of the world's top companies lack the information and processes necessary to respond properly to changes in their companies and their markets.[1]

- **Be flexible**

  As you proceed with your analytics strategy, you'll want to determine whether it improves your business. If measuring one area doesn't make a difference, choose another one. But don't change the strategy too frequently, for that will lead to confusion. Once you reach your goal, you should also reexamine the plan. Remember that implementing analytics is an iterative process. You'll tweak your plan as you go.

Bringing Your Team on Board

Change, no matter how beneficial to a company, is difficult. The increased monitoring made possible by cloud-based analytics may make some employees uncomfortable. Your IT people may worry that they're losing responsibility and authority—after all, you're basically outsourcing your previously on-premise software to an outside third party. Salespeople, too, may resist sharing their valuable customer contact information—even though that data belongs to the company.

Other issues may arise. Perhaps your analytics turns up something surprising. For example, if your company has spent most of its advertising dollars on Internet ads over the past 10 years and you discover that your TV and radio campaigns actually produced a better ROI, you may face pushback from senior managers who want to protect their "sacred cows."

Be understanding of the anxiety that may be triggered by the increased transparency and accountability that analytics offers—but be firm. After all, you'll have the numbers on your side.

1. "Gartner Reveals Five Business Intelligence Predictions for 2009 and Beyond," Gartner, January 15, 2009, http://www.gartner.com/it/page.jsp?id=856714.

worksheet:

Your Analytics Strategy

Fill out this worksheet to figure out a regular schedule of analytics you want to gather. Use the top row as an example.

AREA TO MEASURE	INTEGRATE WITH	WHO RUNS THE REPORTS?	FREQUENCY OF ANALYTICS	SHARE INFORMATION WITH	SHARE INFORMATION WHEN	SHARE INFORMATION HOW
sales	supply mgmt., finance	VP of sales admin.	biweekly	heads and middle managers of sales, supply mgmt., and finance	immediately	upload reports to cloud-based project mgmt. application

CLOUD FILE: INSIDER INSIGHT

Q *What's an unsung benefit of moving to the cloud?*

A Many small and medium businesses do not truly understand the ROI of moving to the cloud. The pay-as-you-grow pricing model is a new concept and can leave many feeling as though the total cost is unknown and can get to be very large. In reality, moving to the cloud can reduce the total cost of ownership of business applications by more than 50 percent.

Q *What causes cloud hesitation and how do you address it?*

A Small and medium businesses want to move to the cloud, but struggle with understanding where to start. Growing companies see that modern cloud applications deliver far greater functionality than legacy solutions, but they don't want to make drastic, sweeping changes and incur the expense of an all-in-one cloud suite. On the other hand, they don't want to launch stand-alone cloud applications that do not interact with other solutions and create data silos. That's why Dell believes in helping small and medium businesses determine what combination of cloud and on-premise solutions make the most sense for them—and then how to connect those solutions so cross-application data can be used to generate better visibility into business performance.

Q *What should businesses do now to prepare for a move to the cloud?*

A First decide which function in your organization would most benefit from better automation. Most small and medium businesses start by deploying CRM in the cloud as the productivity gains of increasing revenues deliver fast ROI.

Q *What will a typical small or medium IT infrastructure look like in 10 years?*

A Many small and medium businesses have on-premise applications that deliver tremendous value now and will continue to for years to come. It's unrealistic to claim that cloud applications will eliminate all premise-based software. It is more likely that the IT infrastructure of the future will be a blend of cloud and on-premise solutions that are tightly integrated.

What's Ahead in the Cloud for *Your* Business?

By the end of this chapter...

you'll have a good idea of what's around the corner for cloud solutions—and how they'll likely continue to change the way you run your business for years to come.

Staggering Growth Rates Predicted for the Cloud

There's no doubt that cloud adoption is accelerating. A study sponsored by North Bridge, GigaOM, and the 451 Group, which surveyed 417 senior business and IT managers at both cloud vendor and cloud customer companies, predicts that by 2014, cloud revenues will exceed $21 billion annually. This represents an estimated annual growth rate of nearly 70 percent between 2009 and 2014.[1]

Small businesses are expected to be the primary drivers of this growth, as they've been the most aggressive users of cloud services to date. (Small businesses represented 68 percent of the survey's respondents, compared to 14 percent enterprises and 18 percent midsize businesses.[2])

---

1. "The Future of Cloud Computing 2011," The Future of Cloud Computing Forum, 2011, http://www.futurecloudcomputing.net/2011-future-cloud-computing-survey-results.

2. Ibid.

Although 40 percent of companies using cloud applications today consider themselves in the "experimenting" phase, 75 percent of respondents said they expect two-thirds of their business applications will reside in the cloud within five years.[3] Interestingly, they anticipate that the business challenges driving them to the cloud will change dramatically over the next five years. Currently, most businesses adopt cloud applications to achieve greater agility, but that goal drops by nearly 50 percent in the long term, replaced by (in order of importance) the need to innovate, the need to stay competitive, and the need to improve mobility.[4]

Widespread Adoption and Ongoing Innovation Is Good News for Business Owners

Given this forward trajectory, what can small businesses expect from cloud service providers as the market matures? It's almost all good news. Tomorrow's cloud solutions will offer:

- **More choices**
  Venture capitalists are investing money in startups at rates not seen in more than 10 years.[5] Entrepreneurs, sensing the depth and breadth of the potential cloud marketplace, are jumping in with both feet. As a result, expect to see upstart challenges to cloud pioneers, as well as contenders creating whole new categories of applications and services.

  Today you have a broad range of cloud application options in categories such as CRM, storage and backup, project management, collaboration, and social media. Over the next five years, you can expect a much wider variety of cloud applications to be offered.

---

3. "The Future of Cloud Computing 2011," The Future of Cloud Computing Forum, 2011, http://www.futurecloudcomputing.net/2011-future-cloud-computing-survey-results.

4. Ibid.

5. "Don't call it the next tech bubble—yet," David A. Kaplan, CNN Money, July 11, 2011. http://tech.fortune.cnn.com/2011/07/11/dont-call-it-the-next-tech-bubble-yet/.

- **Greater functionality**

  As with other technologies that have been adopted by businesses over the decades, expect cloud vendors to continuously enhance and improve their offerings. They'll be driven by user demands and requests for "must-have" features, as well as by the sheer competitive nature of the market as startups proliferate.

- **More capacity**

  Since the ability to scale is one of the prime characteristics small businesses look for when evaluating potential cloud service providers, expect vendors to be continuing to up the ante when it comes to the amount of data that can be stored; the number of transactions per second that can be completed; and the number of users that can be accommodated, among other factors.

- **Higher performance**

  Expect performance to continuously improve over time. This trend will be supported by a combination of more efficient applications from cloud vendors and overall improvements in the global telecommunications infrastructure. Be aware, however, that Internet speeds and bandwidth vary considerably from one geographic location to another, and that some barriers to increasing performance will require the participation of governments and global telecom firms as well as the cloud vendors themselves.

- **More mobility**

  You'll see more and more mobile devices being used for business, and more and more cloud applications that can be successfully deployed on ever more powerful and feature-rich devices.

factoid

Worldwide cloud services revenue reached $68.3 billion in 2010, a 16.6 percent increase from 2009's revenue of $58.6 billion, according to Gartner. Gartner anticipates this strong growth to continue through 2014, when it projects worldwide cloud service revenues to reach an astonishing $148.8 billion.[6]

6. "Global Cloud Services Market to Surpass USD 68 Billion in 2010." Information Week, June 22, 2010. http://www.informationweek.in/Cloud_Computing/10-06-22/Global_cloud_services_market_to_surpass_USD_68_billion_in_2010.aspx.

Team Resources:
Roles and Responsibilities for Maximizing Cloud Solutions

Use this worksheet to think about how to organize cloud-minded teams at your company and get the most out of your cloud solutions.

RESPONSIBILITY	TEAM MEMBERS INVOLVED	CURRENT GOALS AND ACTION ITEMS	DATE TO MEET AND REVIEW RESULTS, REVISIT STRATEGY
Analysis of potential new solutions			
Planning use of and strategy for new solutions			
Deployment and data migration			
Training			
Integration and analytics strategy planning			
Communication of analytical data and business intelligence across organization			
Competitive advantage planning			
Future planning			

AUTOMATIC UPDATES: With SaaS applications, upgrades are managed "behind the scenes" and appear automatically the next time your users log on to the system. This eliminates the need for someone in your office to install software or update hardware and ensures that users are always using the most updated versions of the SaaS applications.

TURNKEY END-TO-END CLOUD SERVICES: Services designed to help small and medium-size businesses leverage the power of SaaS applications. For example, as part of Dell Cloud Business Applications, Dell offers comprehensive cloud solutions, including applications, integration, analytics, and support services that can be up and running in days, not weeks.

Create a Plan to Gain the Most from Your Cloud Strategy

To maximize the natural benefits of cloud solutions, create a plan early in your adoption process to evaluate results and plan ways to get more bang for your buck. And revisit that plan often. Schedule regular team meetings—monthly or quarterly—to review current results, gather feedback from employees, and create strategic go-forward plans.

Even if you don't have a dedicated IT manager or a CIO, think about how you can enlist help from key members of your team to keep your cloud strategy evolving. Who can help you stay abreast of emerging solutions? Who's a natural fit for suggesting process improvements and tracking best practices? Who can share insightful analytics across the organization to drive results based on data?

As you know by now, the cloud is a dynamic resource and tool, and you'll want to have a dynamic plan in place to take full advantage of it.

factoid

Forrester Research predicts that the market for Software-as-a-Service will grow from $21.2 billion in 2011 to $92.8 billion in 2016, with businesses of all sized adopting SaaS applications.[7]

Conclusion

Currently, approximately 27 million small businesses are operating in the United States, and more are appearing every month.[8] Each year small businesses create over 65 percent of all new jobs in the United States.[9]

To all these fledgling businesses as well as established ones, perhaps like yours, the cloud offers tremendous benefits. You get to take advantage of the kind of sophisticated solutions that previously only large companies with huge budgets and dozens of dedicated IT workers could afford. You don't need a lot of cash to get started. And you can grow as you need to.

But it's the fact that you can now integrate these exciting new SaaS applications with each other and with more traditional applications that has opened the door into a new world for small and medium business computing. You will truly be able to begin fully reaping the promise of technology and start turning information into knowledge. You'll be able to use that knowledge to make better business decisions. And, best of all, those decisions will allow you to maximize profitability and growth while minimizing costs and risk.

Welcome to the future of powerful and easy-to-use tools for your business. Welcome to the cloud.

7. "Cloud computing market: $241 billion in 2020," ZDNet, Larry Dignan, April 22, 2011, http://www.zdnet.com/blog/btl/cloud-computing-market-241-billion-in-2020/47702.

8. "Statistics about Business Size (including Small Business)," U.S. Census Bureau, August 3, 2011, http://www.census.gov/econ/smallbus.html.

9. "How important are small businesses to the U.S. economy?," SBA.gov, http://www.sba.gov/sites/default/files/files/sbfaq.pdf.

Resources
CLOUD-SERVICE PROVIDERS

CrunchBase
Comprehensive list of currently available cloud-based applications:

http://www.crunchbase.com/tag/saas

Dell Boomi
DATASHEETS, DEMOS, AND WHITE PAPERS

http://www.boomi.com/resources

5-MINUTE DEMO OF CLOUD INTEGRATION IN ACTION

http://marketing.boomi.com/demo.html

CUSTOMER SUCCESS STORIES

http://www.boomi.com/customers

INTEGRATION SOLUTIONS FOR:

Salesforce users

http://www.boomi.com/solutions/salesforce

NetSuite users

http://www.boomi.com/solutions/netsuite

Taleo users

http://www.boomi.com/solutions/taleointegration

SAP users

http://www.boomi.com/solutions/sap

Dell Cloud Business Applications
Dell Cloud Business Applications, a cloud service uniquely packaged to meet the needs of growing companies, delivers trusted, function-specific, integrated SaaS applications along with reporting, analytics, turnkey Dell services, and support.

www.dellcloudapplications.com

SOLUTIONS

A family of integrated cloud applications and services that enable new business processes while leveraging existing software and technology investments

www.dellcloudapplications.com/cloud-solutions

CLOUD-INTEGRATED CRM

www.dellcloudapplications.com/integratedCRM

PRE-PACKAGED AND ADDITIONAL VALUE-ADDED SERVICES

www.dellcloudapplications.com/crm-implementation-services

VIDEOS, DATASHEETS, WHITEPAPERS, AND OTHER MATERIALS

www.dellcloudapplications.com/crm-resources

Salesforce

SALESFORCE AT A GLANCE

www.salesforce.com/resource_center/

HOW TO SUCCEED WITH SALESFORCE CRM

http://success.salesforce.com/

THE SALESFORCE LEARNING CENTER

http://www.salesforce.com/customer-resources/learning-center/#before-you-start

REVIEW SITES FOR CLOUD APPLICATIONS

CNET

http://www.cnet.com

InfoWorld

http://www.infoworld.com

ZDLabs

http://oasis.peterlink.ru/~dap/nnres/misc/data/Benchmarks/12.html

GetApp

http://www.getapp.com/

CLOUD RESEARCH: ARTICLES, WHITE PAPERS, SURVEYS, AND STUDIES

Cloud Trends and Growth and Adoption Rates

AMI PARTNERS

"World Wide Cloud Services Study 2010"

http://www.crn.in/Software-019Aug010-SMB-Cloud-Spending-To-Approach-100-Billion-By-2014.aspx

Summary of AMI's "World Wide Cloud Services Study" on the current and future adoption rates of cloud-based applications by small and medium businesses, as well as the most popular choices of applications.

APPIRIO

"State of the Public Cloud: The Cloud Adopter's Perspective"

http://thecloud.appirio.com/StateofthePublicCloudWhitepaper1.html

Survey of IT decision makers at 150+ North American companies, all with more than 500 employees, who have already adopted at least one leading SaaS or cloud application. White paper reports why they adopted cloud solutions and the results they have experienced.

GARTNER RESEARCH

"Gartner Executive Programs Worldwide Survey of More Than 2,000 CIOs Identifies Cloud Computing as Top Technology Priority for CIOs in 2011."

http://www.gartner.com/it/page.jsp?id=1526414

Gartner surveyed over 2,000 CIOs regarding their budget plans of for 2011. Cloud computing emerged as the top priority.

INFORMATION WEEK

"Global Cloud Services Market to Surpass USD 68 Billion in 2010"

http://www.informationweek.in/Cloud_Computing/10-06-22/Global_cloud_services_market_to_surpass_USD_68_billion_in_2010.aspx

Summary of Gartner's predictions for cloud services growth in 2010. Findings include information on adoption by enterprises, the sizes of markets in various regions worldwide, and the sectors most likely to adopt cloud services.

MORGAN STANLEY RESEARCH GLOBAL

"Cloud Computing Takes Off: Market Set to Boom as Migration Accelerates"

http://www.morganstanley.com/views/perspectives/cloud_computing.pdf

Morgan Stanley's in-depth study into cloud computing—the drivers behind it, the effects of adoption, and predictions for the future.

Security

ENISA

"Cloud Computing: Benefits, Risks, and Recommendations for Information Security."

http://www.enisa.europa.eu/act/rm/files/deliverables/cloud-computing-risk-assessment

An in-depth analysis of the security risks and benefits of cloud computing that outlines 35 common security risks of cloud services, as well as strategies for mitigating them. The report makes recommendations for comparing cloud vendors security policies and obtaining the necessary assurances that the vendor is secure.

NATIONAL INSTITUTE OF STANDARDS AND TECHNOLOGY (NIST)

"Guidelines on Security and Privacy in Public Cloud Computing"

http://csrc.nist.gov/publications/nistir/ir7751/nistir-7751_2010-csd-annual-report.pdf

This annual report from the Computer Security Division of the NIST provides best practices to ensure information security.

PRICEWATERHOUSECOOPERS

"Global State of Information Security Survey"

http://www.pwc.com/gx/en/information-security-survey

Survey across 130 countries of more than 12,000 C-level executives responsible for IT and security investments studied trends for funding security initiatives.

WHITE HAT SECURITY

"Measuring Website Security: Windows of Exposure"

https://www.whitehatsec.com/resource/whitepapers/cloud.html

White paper that outlines the various security considerations as more and more businesses move their crucial functions to the cloud. Provides guidelines and recommendations.

ISO 27002

http://www.27000.org/iso-27002.htm

The title of this standard is "Information technology. Security techniques. Code of practice for information security management." The ISO 27002 standard encompasses hundreds of options for security management.

Acknowledgments

Many talented people contributed their hard work and expertise to create this book. Fortunately, I work with an amazing team, and a great many people offered their knowledge and insights to help us better understand the real-life benefits and challenges of the cloud. I'd like to thank them all, and in particular:

Alice LaPlante, co-author and researcher. Alice has worked with me and PlanningShop for many years. She's not only an outstanding writer, she's a pleasure to have as a colleague. She's fast, capable, smart, and knowledgeable. And now, she's also a *New York Times* best-selling author with her novel, *Turn of Mind*. Congratulations, Alice!

Anne Marie Bonneau, writer, editor, researcher. Like Alice, Anne Marie is an outstanding writer, a detailed editor, and a thorough researcher. Not only is Anne Marie our resident Canadian, she's a deadpan storyteller who makes everyone laugh.

Rebecca Gaspar, managing editor. Rebecca is the overall manager and 'conductor' of this project and most PlanningShop projects. She is responsive, intelligent, even-tempered, talented—what more can I say? That she loves books? That she teaches yoga and brings her yoga calmness to our projects? Yes, I can say all that and much, much more.

Diana Russell, designer and project manager. Diana has not only managed the timeline and juggled the many moving parts of this project, but she beautifully designed both the interior and exterior of this book. Her design skill has made this book—like so many PlanningShop books—a joy to look at and easier to read. We're glad to have Diana back in the Bay Area so we can work even more closely with her.

Mark Woodworth, copy editor and proofreader. "Eagle eye" Mark is thorough, fast, and easy to work with. Mark's our "no problem" man because he's flexible with tight deadlines, shifting schedules, and last-minute changes. All "no problem."

Rosa Whitten, PlanningShop's office manager, and **Bryan Murray**, our academic manager. Rosa managed all of the administrative details and support for this substantial project as well as serving, along with Bryan, to bring "fresh eyes" to reading the manuscript. They help keep everything running along smoothly and their commitment and enthusiasm makes every day at work a pleasure.

Bill Odell and **Helen Shaughnessy**, from the Dell Cloud Business Applications team. Bill is an experienced Silicon Valley leader, and he not only loves technology, but he is firmly and fervently committed to helping small and medium businesses leverage technology to grow and thrive. Helen has been a strategic contributor, speedy reviewer, and intelligent guide throughout this project. Both have been an absolute joy to work with.

Dell's subject matter experts: Rene Chan (security), Ken Forbes (analytics), JoAnne Ravielli (data migration), and Boomi founder and CTO Rick Nucci (integration). We were so fortunate that Dell made a range of highly experienced subject matter experts available to us— that we both interviewed for this book and turned to for technical details. These are folks who work with cloud solutions in-depth, day in and day out, so they bring deep and real understanding of cloud applications and integration.

Success story subjects: Paul Leary of Blackbird Vineyards, Diane Campos of ISYS, Richard Giddey of StorageCraft, and Marnie Webb of TechSoup. These business leaders shared their real-life experiences of their journey to the cloud—their successes and challenges. Their insight adds greatly to the value and power of this book, and we thank them for their willingness to share their time and their stories with us.

Insider Insight contributors: Ryan Nichols of Appirio, Jon Miller of Marketo, Treb Ryan of OpSource, Anneke Seley of Phone Works, Naveen Agarwal of Pricelock, Michael Radovancevich of Taleo, and, once again, Bill Odell of Dell Cloud Business Applications. These folks are on the front lines of the cloud explosion—representing a wide variety of cloud solutions. They've worked with thousands of clients, and their experiences help illuminate the range of issues, successes, and challenges as businesses embrace the cloud.

Dell's corporate team: Michael Dell and PR experts Jennifer J. Davis, Jillian Fisher, and Christina Furtado. Finally, we are very grateful to the unfailing support and assistance we have received from Dell team members in Round Rock, Texas. The public relations team will help us bring the content of this book—and the opportunities of the cloud—to many small and medium businesses.

Thank you all!

Index

A

Accept 360, 98
Access
  in cloud computing, 34–35, 42–44
    employee rights in, 66
    questions to ask about, 45
    remote, 105
  to information, 35, 135
  to the Internet, 6, 7, 24, 34–35,
    43–44
Accounting, 21
ACT!, 20, 55
Actuate, 96
Affordability, 126
Agarwal, Naveen, 120
Agility, 97
Amazon Web Services, 73
American Airlines Sabre reservation
    system, 124
American Institute of Certified Public
    Accountants, development
    of Statement on Auditing
    Standards No. 70, 68
Analytics, 135–148
  data needs in, 141
  flexibility in, 146
  gaining competitive edge with, 36
  improving business performance
    with, 127, 140
  performing regular reviews in, 145
  planning in, 140, 145–146
  power of combining cloud
    integration with cloud-based,
    136–138
  strategy in, 147
  team involvement in, 146
  transparency in, 135
Android, 33
AOL, 20
Appirio, 57–58
Application programming interfaces
    (APIs), 116, 124
Application purchase price, 81
ARPANET, 9, 18
AT&T, 31
Authentication, 64
  two-factor, 61
Authorization, 61, 64
  setting proper levels of, 64–65
Author Solutions, 57
Auto alert, 36

Automated mailing list management,
    26
Automatic updates, 153

B

Bandwidth, 52
Basecamp, 23, 98
Bell, Alexander Graham, 31
Benioff, Marc, 21
Best-of-breed approach to solutions, 23
Blackbird Vineyards, 35, 116, 140,
    142–143
Bug, use of term, 44
Business
  assessing actual needs of, 90–94
  creating processes that streamline,
    113, 115
  data integration in, 56
  identifying challenges in, 95
  identifying priorities in, 27
  improving performance of, with
    analytics, 140
  making better decisions in, 92–93
  privacy and security concerns of,
    21, 42, 59–74
  real-time alerts in a, 38–39
  technology in transforming, 1–2
  use of cloud computing, 9, 12–13
  visibility and transparency in, 36
Business-centric look at cloud ROI, 85
Business intelligence, 96
  defined, 137

C

Call-per-cost report, 39
Callture, 98
Campos, Diane, 102, 130–131
Capacity, 151
Capital expenditure, 77
Capital expenses, transforming, to
    operational expenses, 13
Capital investment, upfront, 30
CaseTracker, 130
Cash flow, improving, 91
Cast Iron systems, 124
Cell phones, modems on, 44
Change, being sensitivity to difficulty
    of, 110
Checklists. *See also* Worksheets
  Can You Benefit from the Cloud?,
    14

Health Insurance Portability and
    Accountability Act (HIPAA),
    67, 68
Homework, doing your, 99–100, 102
Hotmail, 20, 25, 51
Hubspot, 98
Human resources, 97
HyperOffice, 97

I

IBM, 118
IBM 726, 118
Improvement, soliciting and
    implementing ideas for, 118
Industry-specific software, 49
Information. *See also* Data
    access to, 35, 135
    amount of, in global universe, 128
    outsourcing of, 8–9
    personally identifiable, 67
Information technology (IT)
    future of infrastructure, 73, 88,
        108, 120, 148
    outsourcing of, 8–9
InfoWorld, 100, 156
Infrastructure, 8
    costs of, 31
    investing in, 13
Infrastructure as a Service (IaaS), 8
Insolvency, vulnerability to, 52
Integration, 121–134
    affordability in, 126
    benefits of cloud-based, 124–128
    clarifying needs in, 132–133
    cost-per-call report and, 39
    of data, 35
    defined, 122
    ease of, 19
    flexibility in, 126–127
    globality in, 127–128
    importance of strategy to success
        of, 121
    with other business data, 56
    paying for, 129
    personnel in, 129
    planning strategy for, 128–129
    power of combining, with cloud-
        based analytics, 136–138
    reasons for taking advantage of, 127
    scalability in, 126–127
    third-party, 129
    user friendliness and, 124
    working of, across a variety of
        applications, 122–124

Intergalactic computer network, 9
Internal resistance to cloud computing,
    53
Internet access, 6, 7, 24, 34–35
    importance of, 43–44
Intuit, 51, 96, 97
    Online Payroll, 51
Inventory management, 11, 97–98
iOS, 33
ISO 27002, 68
ISYS, 102, 130–131
IT. *See* Information technology (IT)

L

Layer7tech, 124
Leary, Paul, 35, 116, 140, 142–143
Leasing, 76–77
    defined, 77
LEO (Lyons Electronic Office), 136
License server, 80
Licensing, 76–77
Licklider, J.C. R., 9
Live, going, 118
Lock in, 58
LogMeln, 78
Lotus Notes, 58
Lyons, J., 136

M

Main frames, 6
Maintenance fees, 81
Ma(i)sony Napa Valley, 142, 143
Management control, 36, 38–39
Marketing, 21
Marketing automation, 98
Marketo, 88, 98
Mark II computer, 44
McCarthy, John, 2
Mean time between failures (MTBF),
    43
Mean time to recovery (MTTR), 43
MeetUp, 23
Microsoft, 98
    acquisition of Hotmail, 51
    Office, 20, 77
    update of Office Suite, 81
Microsoft Windows, 28
Miller, Jon, 88
Mobile productivity, 29
Mobility, 151
Morgan Stanley, Alphawise service of,
    83
Multitenancy, 30